Wenham Tea House Cookbook

Wenham Village Improvement Society
Wenham, Massachusetts

COVER: "At the sign of the Tea Kettle and Tabby Cat" welcomed patrons to the first Tabby Cat Tea House and later hung from the corner of the new Wenham Tea House. The sign now decorates the wall of the main dining room.
Art by Jeannie Westra.

PAGE 1: The "new" Wenham Tea House, built in 1916 with the first addition in 1925, is one of two buildings which houses the businesses of the Wenham Village Improvement Society. Funds raised go toward the philanthropic endeavors of the WVIS.

The Wenham Village Improvement Society, Inc., founded in 1893 and incorporated in 1913, is a non-profit civic and philanthropic organization dedicated to the beautification and betterment of the town of Wenham.
Art by Jeannie Westra.

PHOTOGRAPHS: B. H. Conant Collection, Wenham Museum; Lee Nelson, Wenham; Margaret MacNamara, Wenham; Warren Johnson, Wenham; Charles Darling, Salem, Massachusetts.

LINE ART: Jeannie Westra, Wenham.

Published by: Favorite Recipes® Press
                 P. O. Box 305142
                 Nashville, TN 37230

Printed in the United States of America
First Printing: 1992, 7,000 copies

Copyright © Wenham Village Improvement Society
4 Monument Street, Wenham, MA 01984

Library of Congress Number: 92-25281
ISBN: 0-87197-344-8

TABLE OF CONTENTS

FOREWORD

I t is 3:15 on a winter's afternoon. The early dusk creates a lovely warmth to the lighted Tea House where the kettle's on, water bubbling at a full boil. The kitchen is warm, full of the smells of scones and cinnamon toast—an invitation to a restful interlude in a busy day. From the little harness shop nestled between Hobbs House and The First Church, where luncheon was first served in 1911, to the lovely Tea Room that we now enjoy, food has been a unifying force for the entire business operation of the Wenham Village Improvement Society.

The Wenham Village Improvement Society was formed in 1893 by a small group of women. Its first "improvement" was to spend $8 for six chestnut, two maple and two evergreen trees to beautify the town. Its original purpose to contribute to the welfare of the towns-people has continued through these one hundred years by private effort. Money was first earned by summer garden parties, flower shows and fairs. In 1910 it was decided to give up these methods of securing funds and to start a Women's Exchange and Tea House with the twofold purpose of financing the Society's projects and providing an outlet for the product of the home worker.

Now, in celebration of one hundred years of community service, the Improvement Society is publishing the *Wenham Tea House Cookbook,* which is an offering of tasty fare from the Tea House files, employees, patrons, and friends. This cookbook provides not only a collection of memorable and delectable recipes, but an historical sketch of the Improvement Society, Wenham Exchange and Tea House during this last century of the Town of Wenham's 350 years, which is also being celebrated in 1993.

Barbara G. Clark
Manager, Book Department
Wenham, Massachusetts

4

HISTORY OF THE WVIS

MONUMENT SQUARE—1890. (L to R) Civil War Monument, Hobbs Harness Shop, Wenham Congregational Church, Trolley Car Barn

The year was 1893, Queen Victoria was still on the throne of England and Grover Cleveland occupied the White House. The times were not good and a severe financial panic had gripped the country. Just ahead was the new, unknown 20th century. "Women's lib" had never been heard of, but its spirit was alive and well in Wenham, Massachusetts. A small group of women met and formed the Wenham Village Improvement Society (WVIS). Neither the type of activity nor the name—which sometimes brings a smile—was at all unusual in 1893. There were many such groups, few of which have survived. Among those that did, very few have had the stamina and spirit of the WVIS. That is why we are so proud to celebrate our one hundredth anniversary.

Robinson Spaulding Family Group in front of Hobbs House— 1893

On April 8, 1893, our constitution and by-laws were established. It was moved and voted that "any woman of good repute may become a member of this Society by subscribing to its Constitution and By-laws and the annual payment of 50 cents." The original preamble states: "The object of this Society is to adorn and make more attractive the Town of Wenham. To preserve its natural beauties and enhance the same by planting and cultivating trees, shrubs, etc. and doing such other activities as shall tend to beautify and improve its streets and public grounds." On December 31, 1913 (date of WVIS incorporation), an interest in people was added to our preamble . . . "giving attention to such matters as pertain to the general welfare of the town of Wenham and its inhabitants, and of providing a suitable building and grounds for social meetings for the education, improvement and entertainment of the members of the corporation and the people of said town and vicinity." Today, these still constitute the official purposes of the WVIS.

During the early years, great importance was placed on beautifying Wenham. The WVIS took strong measures to protect the elm trees on Main Street from insects, installed street lights from the Hamilton line to Wenham Lake, planted trees at different locations throughout town, took responsibility for the clean-up of public areas, sign-posted all Wenham streets and town boundaries, provided funds to employ a teacher for summer programs such as basket weaving and sewing, and recognized the necessity for a new school house. The projects undertaken by the WVIS during the early years were numerous . . . always following the guidelines to beautify the Town of Wenham and make it a better place to live.

Of course, all these good deeds could not have been accomplished without fund-raising. Bake sales, garden parties, drama nights, dances, bridge parties, rummage sales and porch sales were the means used to achieve these goals. These fund-raisers were very successful. In August of 1904, one such fair raised $895.63.

*View of
Wenham Neck—
1895*

*Original Wenham
Tea House located
in the former
Hobbs Harness
Shop—1912*

However, it was becoming increasingly clear that the long-cherished dream of the Society to establish a Tea House as the basis of a steady income needed to become a reality. In 1911, Miss Dodge reported that she had found a place, the harness shop beside the Hobbs House, "well adapted and the cost of putting it in condition would be approximately $150, with a monthly rental fee of $5." The Tea House opened on May 29, 1912, and realized sales of $1,371.49 during the first year with a profit of $500. Patrons were able to order cups of tea in a dainty room furnished in green with soft buff walls decorated in an unusual manner with friezes of old time scenes and mottos. This was just the beginning.

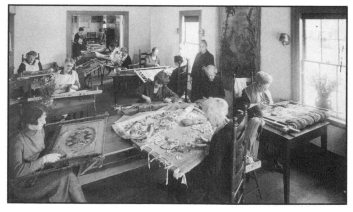

*First rug-making
class of the
Wenham
Exchange—circa
1925*

8

In 1913, it was voted to purchase a plot of land on Monument Street known as the "old Tilton place," at a cost of $2,500 to use as a site for a possible future Tea House. As a result of this purchase, it was necessary to incorporate the Society and revise the Constitution and By-Laws. The date of incorporation was December 31, 1913. In 1916, the Society voted to borrow $5,000 to build the new Tea House and in July of that year the Wenham Tea House opened for business. The building was used as a Community House during the winter months, providing classes in cooking, home nursing, and rug making. In 1918, it was reported that "the House is being constantly used for Committee meetings, Red Cross, Public Safety, WVIS, Food Conservation and churches; magazines from the Public Library are at the House on the days the Library is closed. Many of the summer people who come to Wenham for the different meetings find the Community House a great comfort and convenience as they may have meals and a room when wanted. It is the center of wool distribution for wools for all war knitting and hundreds of pounds are stored in the big summer kitchen."

The WVIS— 1918. Members take part in the Community Cannery for the War Effort.

Claflin-Richards House—1907. Later to become the Wenham Museum

In 1907, WVIS members formed a committee on local history headed by Mrs. Edward B. Cole to "collect and preserve items of interest, items which now exist only in the memory of the older members of the town." As early as 1914, this group considered the possibility of buying the Richards House, one of the oldest houses in Wenham. On November 2, 1921, the WVIS purchased the house partially to provide supplemental space for the Tea House. At this time the Historical Committee was established to "maintain the antiquarian atmosphere of the house."

In 1922, the doll collection of Mrs. Elizabeth Horton, a former resident of the Richards House, was given to the Wenham Historical Committee. In the same year, the Society acquired the photographs of Benjamin H. Conant, an exceptional study of life in Wenham and the surrounding towns in the late 19th and early 20th centuries. These two important collections form the nucleus of the Wenham Museum today.

It became apparent that the Richards House was ill suited to store the doll collection and a new building was required. In 1935, permission was given by the WVIS to borrow up to $2,000 and the "Barn" was built, making use of old timbers and ogee braces which were thought to be part of the 17th-century Third Meetinghouse. On November 10, 1951, ground-breaking ceremonies were held for the Wenham Museum and the renovated "Barn" now known as Burnham Hall. In 1952, the WVIS Historical Committee became the Wenham Historical Association and Museum (Wenham Museum). The WVIS transferred ownership of the Claflin-Richards House, Burnham Hall and all associated properties to the Wenham Museum along with a bequest of Miss Helen C. Burnham for whom the hall was named and a promise for continued financial support. Burnham Hall remains the official meeting place of the WVIS and is also used by town groups and individuals, as well as for activities of the Wenham Museum, such as educational programs, lectures and exhibits. The WVIS continues to make annual financial contributions to support the Wenham Museum and the maintenance of Burnham Hall.

Mary Luscomb House, Main Street, Wenham—1918

In March of 1921, the Society began the long appreciated tradition of Town Meeting Dinner (later Lunch), free to all registered voters. "A full course dinner of roast beef, potatoes and vegetables with pie of your choice" was the fare.

In May of 1944, the WVIS purchased the property of Miss Harriet Hobbs located on the village green beside the Congregational Church. This property included the harness shop which was the site of the original Tea House. After extensive renovations, the "Hobbs House," as it is now called, opened in May of 1948 as an apparel shop.

Perkins Store, Main Street, Wenham —1910. Location of Chadder's Wenham market

The Sports Committee was started in 1924, to develop a skating rink in the swampy area behind the Tea House. The first tennis court was built in 1928 for the benefit of the townspeople. The Enon Tennis Club for adults was formed at this time and the popularity of the game prompted the building of another court in 1934. A third court was added in 1957.

The children of Wenham have always been a top priority in the Society, and summer programs date to 1905. In 1935, the playground was organized to provide summer recreation for all youngsters in town. After the acquisition of the Hobbs property in 1944, the playground area was enlarged. The WVIS still provides a summer playground program and tennis lessons for Wenham children.

On February 8, 1950, it was "voted to allocate $300 annually to be known as the Mandell Memorial Scholarship and to be awarded each year to further the education of one or more boys or girls who are residents of Wenham," as a memorial to Anne and Harriot Mandell. From this modest start, the WVIS Scholarship Fund was established, financed from WVIS income and helped by memorial gifts and donations. The interest from this fund plus annual allotments from WVIS income make this program possible. To date, the WVIS has awarded $404,342 in scholarships to Wenham residents seeking higher education.

Children gathered at the summer playground program—1991

Old Hand Pumper "Enon #1" at the Fire Station—1891

The Society has also participated in many other philanthropies. These include donations toward the purchase of the Trowt land for the new Fire and Police station, the West Wenham tennis court construction, the Civil War Monument fence repairs, donations to the Wenham Museum heating and roof funds, the development of Pleasant Pond Beach, the Enon Village greenhouse, the Cherry Street bike path and walkway, as well as numerous donations to the schools, Little League and other town of Wenham organizations.

The Wenham Tea House, Exchange and Hobbs House directly fund the philanthropic endeavors of the WVIS. The Tea House serves lunch and afternoon tea six days a week. Home-baked gourmet foods, candies and specialty foods are available for purchase. The Exchange offers unusual gifts, cards, stationery, infant clothing, toys and our newest addition—consignment antiques and collectibles on the Treasure Balcony. The Wenham Exchange Book Shop offers a broad selection of titles and personal attention to special orders. Hobbs House has been a major source of income for many years, offering top-quality women's apparel and personalized service in the tradition of bygone years.

William Porter/Fred Stanton Store, Main Street, Wenham— 1910. Location of Water's Insurance

Each year the Tea House participates in "Christmas in Beautiful Downtown Wenham," sponsored by the Council on Aging, at which a complimentary tea is served to young and old alike. By popular demand, the annual Robert D. Hale Book Review and Tea is now in its fourth year. The Fall Fashion Show, held to capacity audiences in the Tea Room, is professionally organized by our expert Hobbs House staff. The WVIS continues to provide assistance to Town agencies such as recent grants to the Wenham Fire Department for a defribrillator and a rescue boat, a video camera for the Police Department, and a computer for one of the schools.

The Wenham Village Improvement Society takes pride in the work it has accomplished this past century. Through the income from the Wenham Tea House, Exchange and Hobbs House, civic and philanthropic work has been possible. Dedicated volunteers and paid staff alike, in unique combination, have had an important part in making this nonprofit business the success story that it is. As we embark on the next century, we look forward in confidence to continued success and subsequent funds to carry out philanthropic work for the town of Wenham.

Committee Members

Barbara Clark, Rita Kelly, Joanne Maestranzi
Suzanne McCarthy, Margaret McNamara
Dorothy Pierce, Dawn A. Schuster, *Chairman*
Sally Taylor, Jeannie Westra.

Special Thanks To

Mrs. John W. Page, who compiled the first 25 years of WVIS history in 1918, and to Mrs. Rupert H. Crehore and Mrs. Joseph Harrington who, in 1974, updated our history in the publication *Highlights of WVIS History.* Excerpts from this booklet have been included in this brief history of the WVIS.

The wide-spreading umbrellas provide shade on a summer afternoon when the neighbors gather for a cup of tea—1926, now main dining room.

*O*n behalf of the staff at the Wenham Tea House and the members of the Wenham
Village Improvement Society, I invite patrons and
friends to sample these delightful recipes for which
the Tea House has become so well known. Celebrate
and share with us one hundred years of service to
the Town of Wenham.

Dawn A. Schuster

Dawn Schuster, *Director*

Inside the Tabby Cat Tea Room, The Wenham Tea House—1918

B. H. CONANT PHOTO—WENHAM MUSEUM

Main Dining Room,
Wenham Tea House

Fancy Sugars

Tea cupboard at
the Ezra Dodge
House, Walnut
Road, Wenham—
1892

Afternoon Tea at the Wenham Tea House

Tea Time

THE WENHAM TEA HOUSE

Driving along a beautiful stretch of country road in 1910, one would come upon the sign "½ Mile To The Tabby Cat Tea Room."

The building had teakettles on the shutters. The dining room carried out the theme with a tabby cat design on its menus and, in the center of each table, a white centerpiece with a black cat and kettle in cross-stitched pattern was placed.

The walls inside were painted buff color and around the top a most unique stenciled frieze, done in green and white, had designs with appropriate mottos pertaining to the subject of tea.

This mural decoration done by a well-known New York artist, a relative of Henry Wadsworth Longfellow, was lost when the building was sold and moved. It was copied on the walls of the new dining room by Mrs. John Burnham, Jr., but over the years, has been painted over.

The original sign has been restored and is displayed in the dining room.

Source: American Cookery, Vol. XX No. 4, November 1915.

Frieze Mottos

"Unless the water boiling be,
filling the teapot spoils the tea."

"Tea which not even critics criticize."

"If my theme I'm rightly thinking, there
are five good reasons for tea drinking:
    Good Friends
    Good Tea
    Because I'm dry
    Or lest I should be bye-and-bye
    Or any other reason why!"

"Polly put the kettle on and we'll all have tea."

"Take a cup and fill it up and call the neighbors in."

"For the cup that cheers and not inebriates waits on all."

"Hear thou great Anna whom three realms obey
doth sometimes council take and sometimes tea."

First Tea House at the Hobbs Harness Shop. Interior view showing friezes

A BRIEF HISTORY OF TEA

The Chinese were credited with using tea as a beverage 4000 years ago. As the legend goes, a well known Emperor who drank only boiling water one day was fueling his fire with wood from a tea bush and a few leaves accidently fell into the pot. He drank it and liked it, and the rest is history.

Tea was first introduced to Europe in the 16th century. Both France and Germany had brief flings with tea drinking, but it fell out of favor with both. France went back to wine and Germany went back to beer.

Only England and Russia had really taken to drinking tea. The Dutch were a distant third.

In England it became popular in coffeehouses which were frequented by male literary figures. In 1706, Times Coffee Houses, owned by Thomas Twining, began a tea dynasty which is now in its ninth generation.

By the mid 1700s, the tea craze gave rise to "tea gardens" where the fashionable came to take tea, gossip, see and be seen. Tea was served from breakfast until closing time.

Kinds of Tea

There are many varieties of tea, but only three types—black, oolong and green, depending on the length of fermentation. Most teas are grown in Ceylon and India.

TEAS TO BE ENJOYED:

Assam—an unblended black tea from India includes stem and flower.

Darjeeling—a delicately flavored black tea grown in the black hills.

Earl Grey—a blend of tea with a citrus-like aroma.

Flavored Teas—black teas with added flavors such as orange or cinnamon.

Gunpowder Tea—green tea leaves that have rolled into tiny pellets.

Herb Tea—can be made from any part of the root, bark, flower or seed of a variety of plants such as peppermint, sage and camomile.

Tea in America developed much the same as in Europe. The Dutch established tea drinking in New Amsterdam. The British continued after purchasing the city and renaming it New York; the "Tea Garden" became popular, and Americans were heavy tea drinkers until the revolution.

In 1904, tea bags happened accidently when a tea merchant, Thomas Sullivan of New York, sent out samples to customers in little silk bags to market his wares and was surprised when orders came in for the *tea bags.*

Source: The Pleasures of Afternoon Tea, Angela Hynes, Price, Stern, Sloan, L.A. 1987.

Brew a Perfect Cup of Tea

1. Rinse the teapot with hot water.
2. Bring fresh cold water to a full rolling boil.
   (It's important to use cold water as it is full of oxygen.)
3. Use 1 teaspoon of loose tea per person and 1 for-the-pot as the saying goes.

CONCENTRATE METHOD
(Usually used to make large quantities)

1. Bring 1 quart fresh cold water to a full rolling boil.
2. Pour over 2/3 cup loose tea. Cover and let stand for 5 minutes.
3. Stir and strain into a quart pitcher or teapot.
4. Use at room temperature within four hours— do not refrigerate.

To serve, pour 2 tablespoons of concentrate into each cup and serve with hot water. Don't worry if concentrate is cloudy. The tea will clear immediately when water is added.

Makes 25 cups.

SUN TEA

Fill a quart pitcher or glass container with cold tap water. Add 8 to 10 tea bags. Cover and let stand at room temperature in the sun for at least 6 hours to overnight. Remove tea bags and squeeze. Keep covered and refrigerated. Pour into ice-filled glasses and serve.

Robert Hale Book Review Menu

*Bridal shower can be similar
or use different choices of sandwiches and desserts.*

Shortbread	Smoked Salmon Sandwiches
Lemon Bread	Asparagus Roll-Ups
Blueberry Bread	Cucumber Rounds
Date Bread	Egg and Watercress Sandwiches
Lemon Meltaways	
Petite Fours	Mushroom Rolls
Mushroom Meringues	Tiny Cream Puff filled with Salad
Linzor Hearts	

Fancy Fruit Tarts
Frosted Grapes
Chocolate-Covered Strawberries

TEA TIME

The *high tea,* still common in many parts of England, is traditionally the meal eaten when the working class returns from factory and fields before the young children go to bed. This usually consists of a hearty meal and includes meats, breads and cheeses to tide them over until dinner, which is usually served after 8 o'clock.

Afternoon teas started with the aristocracy having sandwiches and cakes served around 5 or 6 o'clock.

For *today's tea,* the general rule is the earlier the tea is served, the lighter the refreshment. From 3 o'clock to 6 o'clock the tea is usually a snack, dainty finger sandwiches, scones, desserts and fresh strawberries.

Tea Packs a Punch

For big parties nothing is better than a fruit punch with a tea base. Tea gives body to the punch without masking the flavors of the other ingredients.

1 quart water
¼ cup loose tea
   or 12 tea bags
1 quart cold water
2 6-ounce cans frozen
   lemonade concentrate
2 6-ounce cans frozen
   limeade concentrate
2 cups cranberry juice cocktail
2 28-ounce bottles of ginger ale

Bring 1 quart water to a boil in saucepan. Remove from heat. Add tea immediately. Cover and brew for 5 minutes. Strain into punch bowl containing 1 quart cold water. Stir in concentrates and cranberry juice. Place block of ice or ice cubes in punch. Add ginger ale just before serving.
Yield: 5 quarts.

*To use instant tea, simply combine ¼ cup tea with 2 quarts cold water in punch bowl. No need to boil water and brew.

Special Tea

Recipes Used in The Tea Room—1926

Toasted Lobster Sandwich

Cut lobster in dice, mix with mayonnaise, put between bread—toast slowly. Butter one side and serve.

Cinnamon Toast

Cut white bread rather thick, toast quickly, butter and sprinkle with cinnamon and sugar which have been mixed together. Serve hot.

Toasted Salmon Sandwiches

Butter bread slightly and sprinkle with shredded smoked salmon, which has been soaked and boiled. Toast, butter one side and serve hot.

Bon Chees

2 cups white flour
2 teaspoons baking
* powder*
1 teaspoon shortening
¼ teaspoon of salt

Mix with milk until a soft dough and cut with biscuit cutter. Bake in hot oven. When cool make a small hole in top of each biscuit and fill with salad of any kind. Garnish with a sprig of lettuce.

Cheese Sandwich

Cream 1 tablespoon butter with 1 tablespoon beef extract. Add salt and pepper. Over this, grate cheese, then spread on thin slices of buttered bread; put into oven until cheese melts.

Tea Tray

Setting a Tea Table

TEA SANDWICHES

There are endless variations of tea sandwiches—use your imagination! (Just remember not to use anything too wet as it will soak into bread.) Different flavors and textures of bread, tiny cream puffs filled with chicken, crab, or lobster salad are always good. Tiny biscuits, puff pastry shells, muffins, tea breads sliced thin and spread with cream cheese.

Cookie cutters also give a wide array of shapes. Remember to keep everything bite-size and dainty and garnish attractively.

Make up a variety of sandwiches and, if they are not to be served immediately, they will hold nicely in refrigerator for a few hours if sealed in airtight plastic bags or with a piece of waxed paper and a slightly damp towel over them.

Put several varieties on serving dish or platter. Dress up platter with parsley, chicory, flowers, vegetables (radish roses, carrot curls, etc.) Color is essential as the visual effect is as important as these tasty morsels.

Rolled tea sandwiches are more time consuming, as they have to be made the day before to create the visual effect that makes them so interesting.

All sandwiches are rolled as tightly as possible, wrapped in waxed paper, and stored in large enough containers so they are not cramped. Cover with a damp paper towel and foil and store overnight in refrigerator. Just before the event, take out and cut.

Bread

1 loaf unsliced day-old
*   white or wheat bread*
1/2 cup softened butter
    Cut all crust off bread. Cut lengthwise into as thin a slice as possible. Spread thinly with butter, then filling. Roll up lengthwise jelly roll fashion. Wrap in waxed paper. Chill, covered with damp paper towel and foil, for 3 hours to overnight. Cut in thin slices.

Tea Sandwich Ideas

FILLINGS FOR ROLLED SANDWICHES

Honey and finely grated orange rind: One tablespoon of each to 3 ounces cream cheese.

Crushed pineapple, well drained, and finely chopped pecans: Add to cream cheese.

Cooked shrimp, mashed with fork: Add to softened cream cheese.

TOPPINGS FOR OPEN-FACED SANDWICHES

Curried chicken with finely chopped walnuts: Chicken salad with small amount curry powder to taste and walnuts.

Shrimp with celery: Small cooked shrimp on buttered round. Sprinkle thinly sliced celery on top. Sprinkle with parsley flakes.

Almond-Chicken filling: 1 cup chopped cooked chicken, 1/4 cup chopped blanched almonds, and 1/2 cup finely chopped celery. Moisten with mayonnaise. Season to taste with lemon juice, salt and pepper. Garnish.

Tomato and Basil: Use black bread. Spread with mayonnaise. Slice tomato thinly. Place slice on bread. Sprinkle with basil. Garnish.

Cream Cheese and Olive

Whole stuffed olives, patted dry
9 ounces cream cheese
  (room temperature)
1/2 cup finely chopped olives
Few drops of cream

Mix together cream cheese, chopped olives and cream to make spreading consistency. Cut crust off sliced wheat or white bread; roll flat with rolling pin. Spread bread with light coating of softened butter, and then the cream cheese mixture. Add 4 whole olives, 1 at each end and 2 evenly spaced in between (face olives lengthwise). Roll and wrap as stated above. The next day, slice off ends, slicing through olive and cut into each olive. Sprinkle with parsley for garnish. Cream cheese and cherry is also done this way.

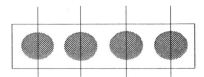

Rolled Asparagus

*1 pound medium size asparagus,
steamed until just crunchy
and peeled. May use canned.*

Drain asparagus on paper towel until moisture is extracted (better to do the day before). It is very important that the asparagus not be too wet. Cut crusts off light texture bread; roll thin. Mix softened butter with a little lemon juice and spread over bread (have bread point facing you). Place 2 spears of asparagus on bread, leaving tip end showing at each end. Sprinkle with a little salt, roll tightly and wrap in waxed paper. Store in refrigerator. Just before serving, cut into 3 pieces. Sprinkle with parsley or paprika.

Mushroom Rolls

*1 large onion, cut fine
2 pounds mushrooms, very finely
    chopped or processed
4 to 5 tablespoons butter
1/2 cup sour cream
1 1/4 teaspoons thyme
1/2 teaspoon salt
2 tablespoons flour*

Melt butter in heavy skillet. Cook mushrooms and onions over medium low heat, stirring frequently for 10 to 12 minutes. Add rest of ingredients and cook down to a paste. Chill. Cut crust off bread; roll flat. Spread thin layer of softened butter over bread (to prevent bread from becoming soggy). Spread with mushroom mixture. Roll tightly. Wrap in waxed paper. Store in refrigerator as stated previously. Next day, cut off ends to remove jagged edges. Cut into 3 to 4 bite-sized pieces. Garnish.

Smoked Salmon Pinwheel Sandwich

*8 ounces smoked salmon
12 ounces softened cream cheese
1 1/2 ounces chives, minced
1 1/2 ounces bacon bits, chopped
4 ounces heavy cream*

Blend all ingredients. Spread on rye or wheat bread. Garnish with dill.

Breadless Roll

*Ham, sliced thin
Cream cheese, softened and
    thinned with milk
    if necessary
Stuffed olives, patted dry*

Spread ham with cream cheese. Place olives lengthwise, spaced evenly apart and roll. Wrap in waxed paper and store in refrigerator. Next day, cut through olives as in Cream Cheese and Olive (page 28). Garnish as desired.

OPEN-FACED SANDWICHES

Cucumber

Cut cucumber very thin. Put in colander. Sprinkle with salt. Let drain. Pat dry on paper towels. Cut bread into rounds using biscuit cutter. Spread a thin layer of softened butter, then mayonnaise over top. Add cucumber. Put tiny dollop of mayonnaise on top. Garnish with sprig of dill.

Dilled Salmon Cream Cheese Spread

3 ounces cream cheese, softened
2 teaspoons milk
1 teaspoon fresh dill
 or ¼ teaspoon dried dillweed
Generous dash freshly ground
 pepper

Mix cream cheese, milk, dill and pepper. With 1¾-inch round cookie cutter, cut rounds from 6 very thin slices pumpernickle bread. Chop salmon. Spread each round with scant teaspoon cream cheese mixture. Top with ½ teaspoon chopped salmon.

Egg and Watercress

1 small bunch watercress,
 washed, drained and pat dry
5 hard cooked eggs
2 tablespoons mayonnaise
Dijon mustard to taste

Coarsely chop ½ of watercress (½ cup lightly packed). Roughly chop eggs with knife. Add mayonnaise and mustard, salt and pepper. Mash to a smooth paste with fork. Stir in chopped watercress until smooth. Use remaining watercress as garnish.

Spread on 3 thin slices of lightly buttered bread. Stack. Cover with fourth slice. Cut off crusts. Refrigerate 1 hour for easier cutting. To serve, cut each sandwich into 6 slices, then cut lengthwise.

To refrigerate: Towel line jelly roll pan. Cover with damp paper towels and plastic wrap. Refrigerate 1 hour or until ready to serve. To serve, cut sandwich into strips or diagonally. Garnish.

Chutney Cream Cheese

4 ounces cream cheese, softened
Chutney to taste
3 tablespoons finely chopped
 walnuts

In a small bowl, stir together the cream cheese, chutney and walnuts until combined. (Use immediately or cover and refrigerate; bring to room temperature to use.) Makes ⅔ cup.

Spread on thinly sliced crustless whole wheat bread and sandwich it with thin slices of apples for crunch. Cut each sandwich diagonally into quarters.

Tuna Capers

1 7-ounce can water-packed
 tuna, drained and flaked
5 tablespoons mayonaise
1 teaspoon lemon juice
Salt and pepper to taste
1 teaspoon capers, finely
 chopped
Chives for garnish

Place tuna in medium bowl and mash to a paste. Stir in mayonnaise and lemon juice. Season with salt and pepper. Stir in capers. Spread. Garnish plate with chives.

Filled Cream Puffs

Follow recipe for cream puffs. Make them very small.

Cut off tops. Mix ¼ cup sour cream and 1½ teaspoons lemon juice together. Fill cream puff with scant teaspoon of mixture. Top with tiny dollop (⅛ teaspoon) caviar in center. Garnish.

TODAY'S TEA HOUSE FAVORITES

Fruit Dip

½ cup packed brown sugar
1 cup sour cream

½ teaspoon vanilla extract

Combine brown sugar, sour cream and vanilla in bowl; beat until smooth. Spoon into serving dish. Serve with whole strawberries, pineapple chunks and banana slices dipped in lemon juice. **Yield: 12 servings.**

Approx Per Serving: Cal 84; Prot 1 g; Carbo 12 g; Fiber 0 g;
    T Fat 4 g; 42% Calories from Fat; Chol 9 mg; Sod 15 mg.

Fruit Compote

1   16-ounce can fruit cocktail,
    drained
8 ounces sour cream

½ cup coconut
½ cup miniature marshmallows

Combine all ingredients in bowl; mix gently. Garnish servings with cherries and pineapple. **Yield: 4 servings.**

Approx Per Serving: Cal 252; Prot 3 g; Carbo 29 g; Fiber 2 g;
    T Fat 15 g; 52% Calories from Fat; Chol 25 mg; Sod 45 mg.

Crème Brûlée

6 egg yolks
⅓ cup sugar
3 cups whipping cream

1 teaspoon vanilla extract
⅓ cup packed brown sugar

Whisk egg yolks with sugar in bowl until very smooth. Heat cream in heavy saucepan over medium heat just until bubbles form around side of saucepan; do not boil. Whisk a small amount of hot mixture into egg yolks; whisk egg yolks gradually into hot mixture. Cook over medium-low heat for 15 minutes or until mixture just coats back of spoon, stirring constantly. Stir in vanilla. Spoon into 1½-quart soufflé dish. Chill for several hours to overnight. Sift brown sugar evenly over chilled custard. Broil for 3 to 4 minutes or until brown sugar melts to form a shiny crust. Chill for 1 to 3 hours. Place dish on serving tray. Arrange fruit such as sliced strawberries, pineapple chunks and banana chunks around dish. Serve Crème Brûlée over fruit. **Yield: 10 servings.**

Approx Per Serving: Cal 343; Prot 3 g; Carbo 17 g; Fiber 0 g;
    T Fat 30 g; 77% Calories from Fat; Chol 226 mg; Sod 36 mg.

Glazed Fruit Tartlets

3 egg yolks, beaten
1/3 cup sugar
2 tablespoons flour
1/2 teaspoon vanilla extract
1 cup milk
1/2 cup butter, softened
1/2 cup sugar
1 egg yolk
1 tablespoon orange juice
1 tablespoon grated orange rind

1 teaspoon vanilla extract
1 3/4 cups flour
1/2 cup sugar
4 1/2 teaspoons cornstarch
Salt to taste
1 cup orange juice
2 teaspoons grated orange rind
1 tablespoon orange liqueur
4 cups drained mandarin
   oranges

Whisk 3 egg yolks with 1/3 cup sugar until smooth. Whisk in 2 tablespoons flour and 1/2 teaspoon vanilla. Bring milk just to a simmer in saucepan. Whisk a small amount of hot milk into egg yolk mixture; whisk egg yolks into hot milk. Bring to a boil, stirring constantly. Cook for 1 minute, stirring constantly. Cool to room temperature. Chill in refrigerator. Beat butter in medium mixer bowl until light. Add 1/2 cup sugar gradually, beating until fluffy. Beat in next 4 ingredients. Mix in 1 3/4 cups flour. Press into 2-inch tartlet cups. Bake at 350 degrees for 15 to 20 minutes or until light brown. Cool in cups for 10 minutes. Loosen carefully with tip of knife; remove to wire rack to cool completely. Mix 1/2 cup sugar, cornstarch and salt in small saucepan. Stir in 1 cup orange juice gradually. Bring to a boil; stirring constantly. Cook for 2 minutes, stirring constantly. Stir in 2 teaspoons orange rind. Cool, covered, to room temperature. Stir in liqueur. Fill tartlets 1/4 full with chilled custard. Top with oranges. Spoon orange glaze over top, covering oranges completely. Chill for up to 8 hours. May substitute bananas, strawberries, drained pineapple chunks or blueberries for oranges. **Yield: 24 servings.**

Approx Per Serving: Cal 156; Prot 2 g; Carbo 26 g; Fiber <1 g;
   T Fat 5 g; 29% Calories from Fat; Chol 47 mg; Sod 38 mg.

Coconut-Date Balls

1 8-ounce package dates,
   chopped
1 cup sugar
1/2 cup margarine
1 egg

Salt to taste
1/2 teaspoon vanilla extract
1/3 cup chopped walnuts
2 cups rice crispies
2 cups coconut

Combine first 5 ingredients in saucepan. Cook over low heat for 10 minutes, stirring constantly. Add vanilla. Cool for 20 minutes. Stir in walnuts and cereal. Shape into 1-inch balls; roll in coconut. Let stand until firm. Refrigerate in airtight container. **Yield: 36 servings.**

Approx Per Serving: Cal 96; Prot 1 g; Carbo 14 g; Fiber 1 g;
   T Fat 5 g; 43% Calories from Fat; Chol 6 mg; Sod 52 mg.

Petits Fours

1¹/₂ cups sifted cake flour
³/₄ cup sugar
1³/₄ teaspoons baking powder
1¹/₂ teaspoons salt
¹/₄ cup shortening

²/₃ cup milk
3 egg yolks
1 teaspoon vanilla extract
Glaze
Frosting

Sift first 4 ingredients into bowl. Add shortening and milk. Beat at low speed for 30 seconds. Beat at medium speed for 2 minutes. Add egg yolks and vanilla. Beat for 1 minute. Spoon into greased and floured 8x11-inch cake pan. Bake at 350 degrees for 20 to 25 minutes or until center springs back when lightly touched. Cool in pan for 10 minutes. Remove to wire rack to cool completely. Wrap in foil. Freeze until firm. Cut crusty edges and top from frozen cake; cut cake into small squares. Place squares on wire rack over waxed paper. Pour hot Glaze over cake squares. Let stand for 1 hour. Spoon Frosting over cake squares. Let stand until dry. Decorate as desired. **Yield: 32 servings.**

Glaze

1 cup sugar
1 cup water

³/₄ cup apricot preserves

Cook sugar and water in saucepan over medium heat until sugar dissolves. Boil for 10 minutes. Cool to room temperature. Bring preserves to a simmer in small saucepan. Press through sieve into bowl. Stir in sugar syrup. Keep warm over hot water.

Frosting

1 cup sugar
1¹/₂ cups water
¹/₄ teaspoon cream of tartar
Salt to taste

4 to 4¹/₂ cups sifted
   confectioners' sugar
¹/₂ teaspoon almond extract

Combine sugar, water, cream of tartar and salt to taste in medium saucepan. Cook over low heat until sugar dissolves, stirring constantly. Cook over medium heat to 226 degrees on candy thermometer; do not stir. Pour into double boiler. Cool to 110 degrees. Beat in enough confectioners' sugar to make a frosting thick enough to coat wooden spoon but thin enough to pour. Stir in almond extract. Keep warm over hot water.

Approx Per Serving: Cal 180; Prot 1 g; Carbo 40 g; Fiber <1 g;
   T Fat 2 g; 11% Calories from Fat; Chol 21 mg; Sod 122 mg.

Lemon Meltaways

3/4 cup butter, softened
3/4 cup sugar
1/4 cup milk
1 egg
1 tablespoon lemon juice
Grated rind of 1 large lemon

1/2 teaspoon vanilla extract
2 cups flour
1 teaspoon baking powder
1/4 teaspoon baking soda
1/4 teaspoon salt
1 cup sugar

Cream butter and 3/4 cup sugar in mixer bowl until light and fluffy. Beat in milk and egg. Add lemon juice, lemon rind and vanilla; mix well. Sift flour, baking powder, baking soda and salt into bowl. Add to creamed mixture 1/3 at a time, mixing well after each addition. Chill, covered, for 2 hours or until firm. Shape into 1/2-inch balls; roll in 1 cup sugar. Place 2 inches apart on lightly greased cookie sheet. Bake at 350 degrees for 8 minutes or until edges are light brown. Remove to wire rack to cool. Store in airtight container in cool place for up to 2 weeks or freeze. **Yield: 72 servings.**

Approx Per Serving: Cal 50; Prot <1 g; Carbo 8 g; Fiber <1 g;
T Fat 2 g; 36% Calories from Fat; Chol 8 mg; Sod 33 mg.

Meringue Mushrooms

1/4 cup egg whites
Salt to taste
2 tablespoons sugar
2 tablespoons confectioners'
  sugar

1/4 teaspoon egg white
1 tablespoon confectioners'
  sugar
1 teaspoon baking cocoa

Beat 1/4 cup egg whites with salt in mixer bowl for 1 minute. Add mixture of sugar and 2 tablespoons confectioners' sugar 1/3 at a time, mixing for 20 seconds after each addition. Beat until mixture is stiff and glossy. Spoon into pastry bag fitted with 1/2-inch plain tip. Pipe into fifteen 1/2 to 1-inch domed mounds for mushroom caps on baking sheet lined with baking parchment. Pipe fifteen 1/2 to 1-inch high peaked mounds for mushroom stems. Bake at 150 degrees for 1 3/4 hours or until meringues are dry and just begin to color. Let stand until completely cool. Mix 1/4 teaspoon egg white with 1 tablespoon confectioners' sugar in small bowl. Cut small hole in bottom of each mushroom cap with small sharp knife. Dip peaked end of stem pieces into confectioners' sugar mixture. Push gently into holes in mushroom caps. Store in airtight container for up to 1 day. Dust with baking cocoa at serving time. Use to garnish Bûche de Noël. **Yield: 15 mushrooms.**

Approx Per Mushroom: Cal 14; Prot <1 g; Carbo 3 g; Fiber <1 g;
T Fat <1 g; 1% Calories from Fat; Chol 0 mg; Sod 5 mg.

Linzer Hearts

1½ cups unsalted butter,
  softened
1 cup confectioners' sugar
1 egg
2 cups unbleached flour, sifted

1 cup cornstarch
2 cups finely ground walnuts
½ cup red raspberry preserves
¾ cup confectioners' sugar

Cream butter and 1 cup confectioners' sugar in mixer bowl until light and fluffy. Beat in egg. Sift in flour and cornstarch; mix well. Mix in walnuts. Chill, wrapped in waxed paper, for 4 to 6 hours. Roll ¼ inch thick on lightly floured surface. Cut with 1½-inch heart cutter; place on ungreased cookie sheet. Chill for 45 minutes. Bake at 325 degrees for 10 to 15 minutes or until light brown. Remove to wire rack. Spread half the warm cookies with jam; top with remaining cookies. Sift ¾ cup confectioners' sugar into bowl. Press tops and bottoms of cookies into confectioners' sugar. Cool completely on wire rack. **Yield: 48 servings.**

Approx Per Serving: Cal 137; Prot 1 g; Carbo 13 g; Fiber <1 g;
  T Fat 9 g; 58% Calories from Fat; Chol 20 mg; Sod 3 mg.

Pecan Tasties

3 ounces cream cheese, softened
½ cup butter, softened
1 cup flour
1 egg
1 tablespoon butter, softened

¾ teaspoon baking soda
Salt to taste
1 teaspoon vanilla extract
⅔ cup chopped pecans

Combine cream cheese, ½ cup butter and flour in bowl; mix well. Chill in refrigerator. Shape into balls. Press into miniature tart cups. Combine egg, 1 tablespoon butter, baking soda, salt, vanilla and pecans in bowl; mix well. Spoon into tart shells. Bake at 350 degrees for 20 to 25 minutes or until set. Remove to wire rack to cool. **Yield: 16 servings.**

Approx Per Serving: Cal 142; Prot 2 g; Carbo 7 g; Fiber 1 g;
  T Fat 12 g; 75% Calories from Fat; Chol 37 mg; Sod 113 mg.

Fluted Mushroom—Select firm, round white mushrooms. Rub gently with lemon juice to prevent discoloration. Press the flat tip of a knife into the center of the mushroom cap in a star design. Continue making indentations in rows around mushroom cap.

Shortbread

1 cup butter, softened
1/2 cup confectioners' sugar,
  sifted

2 cups sifted flour

Cream butter in mixer bowl until light. Add confectioners' sugar, beating until fluffy. Add flour; knead until smooth. Roll 1/4 inch thick on lightly floured surface. Place on cookie sheet. Bake at 350 degrees for 18 to 20 minutes or until light golden brown. Remove to wire rack to cool. Cut into wedges to serve. **Yield: 16 servings.**

Approx Per Serving: Cal 173; Prot 2 g; Carbo 16 g; Fiber <1 g;
  T Fat 12 g; 60% Calories from Fat; Chol 31 mg; Sod 97 mg.

Thimble Cookies

1 egg yolk
1/2 cup margarine, softened
1/4 cup sugar
1 teaspoon vanilla extract
1 cup sifted flour

1/2 teaspoon salt
2 egg whites, slightly beaten
1 cup finely chopped pecans
1/4 cup raspberry jelly

Combine egg yolk, margarine, sugar and vanilla in mixer bowl; mix well. Add flour and salt; mix well. Shape into small balls. Dip in egg whites; roll in pecans. Place on cookie sheet. Bake at 350 degrees for 5 minutes. Press center of each cookie with finger or spoon to make indentation. Bake for 5 minutes longer. Remove to wire rack. Fill indentations with jelly. Let stand until cool. **Yield: 24 servings.**

Approx Per Serving: Cal 105; Prot 1 g; Carbo 9 g; Fiber <1 g;
  T Fat 7 g; 62% Calories from Fat; Chol 9 mg; Sod 94 mg.

Fluted Fruit Wheels—Cut thin strips of rind evenly from stem end to blossom end of lemons, oranges and limes. Cut fruit into slices of desired thickness. To make twists, cut from 1 side to center and twist. For fans, cut fruit into slices, cutting to but not through bottom side; fan out slices.

Lemon-Blueberry Bread

3/4 cup sugar
1/2 cup milk
1/4 cup unsalted butter, softened
1 egg
2 cups unbleached flour

2 teaspoons baking powder
1/4 teaspoon salt
2 cups fresh blueberries
1 tablespoon grated lemon rind
Topping

Combine sugar, milk, butter and egg in medium bowl; stir until smooth. Add mixture of flour, baking powder and salt; mix until moistened. Fold in blueberries and lemon rind. Spoon into greased 5x9-inch loaf pan. Sprinkle Topping over batter. Bake at 375 degrees for 50 minutes or until topping is golden brown and crusty. Remove to wire rack to cool.
Yield: 12 servings.

Topping

1/2 cup sugar
1/3 cup unbleached flour
1/4 cup unsalted butter, softened

1 teaspoon grated lemon rind
1/2 teaspoon cinnamon

Combine sugar, flour, butter, lemon rind and cinnamon in small bowl; mix well.

Approx Per Serving: Cal 253; Prot 3 g; Carbo 41 g; Fiber 1 g;
T Fat 9 g; 31% Calories from Fat; Chol 40 mg; Sod 113 mg.

Carrot Bread

1 cup sugar
3/4 cup oil
2 eggs
1 teaspoon vanilla extract
1 1/2 cups sifted flour

1 tablespoon baking powder
1 teaspoon salt
1 teaspoon cinnamon
1 cup grated carrots
1/2 cup chopped walnuts

Combine sugar and oil in mixer bowl. Beat until smooth. Beat in eggs 1 at a time. Add vanilla and mixture of flour, baking powder, salt and cinnamon; mix well. Fold in carrots and walnuts. Spoon into greased 5x9-inch loaf pan. Bake at 350 degrees for 1 hour or until bread tests done. Remove to wire rack to cool. **Yield: 12 servings.**

Approx Per Serving: Cal 287; Prot 3 g; Carbo 30 g; Fiber 1 g;
T Fat 18 g; 55% Calories from Fat; Chol 36 mg; Sod 276 mg.

Cranberry-Orange Bread

2 cups sifted flour
1 cup sugar
1½ teaspoons baking powder
½ teaspoon baking soda
½ teaspoon salt
2 tablespoons shortening

Juice and grated rind of 1
  orange
1 egg, beaten
1 cup cranberries, cut into
  halves

Sift flour, sugar, baking powder, baking soda and salt into large bowl. Cut in shortening until crumbly. Combine orange juice and orange rind in 1-cup measure. Add enough water to measure ¾ cup. Add to crumb mixture with egg; mix well. Fold in cranberries. Spoon into greased 5x9-inch loaf pan. Bake at 350 degrees for 1 hour or until wooden pick inserted in center comes out clean. Remove to wire rack to cool. **Yield: 12 servings.**

Approx Per Serving: Cal 168; Prot 3 g; Carbo 33 g; Fiber 1 g;
    T Fat 3 g; 15% Calories from Fat; Chol 18 mg; Sod 171 mg.

Date Bread

1 cup chopped dates
2 tablespoons butter
1 cup boiling water
1 teaspoon baking soda
1 egg
⅓ cup sugar

⅓ cup packed brown sugar
2½ cups flour
1 teaspoon baking powder
¼ teaspoon salt
1 cup coarsely chopped walnuts

Combine dates, butter, water and baking soda in medium bowl; mix well and set aside. Beat egg until frothy in large mixer bowl. Beat in sugar and brown sugar. Mix flour, baking powder and salt together. Add to sugar mixture alternately with date mixture, mixing just until moistened after each addition. Stir in walnuts. Spoon into greased and floured 5x9-inch loaf pan. Bake at 350 degrees for 1 hour or until bread tests done. Cool in pan for 5 minutes. Remove to wire rack to cool completely. May bake in three 3x5-inch loaf pans for 35 to 40 minutes if preferred. **Yield: 12 servings.**

Approx Per Serving: Cal 273; Prot 5 g; Carbo 46 g; Fiber 3 g;
    T Fat 9 g; 28% Calories from Fat; Chol 23 mg; Sod 168 mg.

Lemon Bread

1/3 cup shortening
1 cup sugar
2 eggs
1/2 cup milk
Grated rind of 2 lemons

1 1/2 cups flour
1 teaspoon baking powder
1/2 teaspoon salt
Juice of 1 lemon
1/4 cup sugar

Cream shortening and 1 cup sugar in mixer bowl until light and fluffy. Beat in eggs, milk and lemon rind. Add mixture of flour, baking powder and salt; mix just until moistened. Spoon into greased loaf pan. Bake at 350 degrees for 1 hour. Blend lemon juice with 1/4 cup sugar in bowl. Pour over hot bread. Cool in pan for several minutes. Remove to wire rack to cool completely. May double recipe to make 2 loaves. **Yield: 12 servings.**

Approx Per Serving: Cal 208; Prot 3 g; Carbo 34 g; Fiber <1 g;
     T Fat 7 g; 30% Calories from Fat; Chol 37 mg; Sod 133 mg.

Pumpkin Bread

4 eggs
1 1/4 cups oil
2 cups sugar
2 cups mashed cooked pumpkin
3 cups flour
2 teaspoons baking powder

1 1/2 teaspoons baking soda
1 tablespoon cinnamon
1 teaspoon nutmeg
1 teaspoon salt
2 cups raisins
1 cup chopped walnuts

Beat eggs in mixer bowl. Add oil, sugar and pumpkin; beat until smooth. Sift flour, baking powder, baking soda, cinnamon, nutmeg and salt together. Add to egg mixture; mix well. Stir in raisins and walnuts. Spoon into 2 greased loaf pans. Bake at 350 degrees for 1 hour. Remove to wire rack to cool. **Yield: 24 servings.**

Approx Per Serving: Cal 312; Prot 4 g; Carbo 42 g; Fiber 2 g;
     T Fat 16 g; 44% Calories from Fat; Chol 36 mg; Sod 182 mg.

 Strawberry Fans—Select large firm strawberries with caps. Cut several parallel slices from the tip of each berry to just below the cap with sharp knife. Spread slices gently to form fan.

Zucchini Bread

2 eggs, beaten
1 cup oil
2 cups sugar
1 tablespoon vanilla extract
3 cups flour

1/4 teaspoon baking soda
1 teaspoon baking powder
1 tablespoon cinnamon
1 teaspoon salt
2 cups grated unpeeled zucchini

Beat eggs with oil, sugar and vanilla in mixer bowl. Add flour, baking soda, baking powder, cinnamon and salt; mix well. Stir in zucchini. Spoon into 2 greased loaf pans. Bake at 325 degrees for 1 hour. Remove to wire rack to cool. May add 1/2 cup nuts if desired. **Yield: 24 servings.**

Approx Per Serving: Cal 211; Prot 2 g; Carbo 29 g; Fiber 1 g;
T Fat 10 g; 41% Calories from Fat; Chol 18 mg; Sod 104 mg.

Cheddar Dill Scones

2 1/2 cups flour
1 cup shredded Cheddar cheese
1/4 cup chopped fresh parsley
1 tablespoon baking powder
2 teaspoons dillweed

1/2 teaspoon salt
3/4 cup butter
2 eggs, slightly beaten
1/2 cup half and half

Combine flour, cheese, parsley, baking powder, dillweed and salt in bowl. Cut in butter until crumbly. Add eggs and half and half; mix just until moistened. Knead for 1 minute on lightly floured surface. Divide into halves. Roll each portion into 8-inch circle; cut each into 8 wedges. Place 1 inch apart on baking sheet. Bake at 400 degrees for 10 to 15 minutes or until light brown. **Yield: 16 servings.**

Approx Per Serving: Cal 197; Prot 5 g; Carbo 16 g; Fiber 1 g;
T Fat 13 g; 58% Calories from Fat; Chol 60 mg; Sod 257 mg.

Green Onion Frills—Cut off root end and most of stem portion of green onions. Make narrow lengthwise cuts at both ends with sharp knife to produce a fringe. Chill in iced water until ends curl.

Cran-Orange Scones

1/2 cup chopped fresh or frozen
  cranberries, drained
2 tablespoons sugar
2 cups flour
1/4 cup sugar
2 teaspoons baking powder
1/2 teaspoon salt
1/2 cup unsalted butter, chilled

2 eggs
2 tablespoons orange juice
1/2 teaspoon grated orange rind
1 teaspoon vanilla extract
1/2 cup chopped pecans
1 egg white
1/2 teaspoon water

Butter a 10-inch circle in center of baking sheet. Combine cranberries and 2 tablespoons sugar in small bowl; mix well. Let stand for 5 minutes. Mix flour, 1/4 cup sugar, baking powder and salt in large bowl. Cut in butter until crumbly. Beat eggs, orange juice, orange rind and vanilla in small bowl until smooth. Add to dry ingredients; stir until moistened. Knead in cranberries and pecans to distribute evenly; dough will be sticky. Pat into 9-inch circle on buttered circle on baking sheet. Brush with mixture of egg white and water. Cut into 8 wedges with serrated knife. Bake at 400 degrees for 20 minutes or until wooden pick comes out clean. **Yield: 8 servings.**

Approx Per Serving: Cal 331; Prot 10 g; Carbo 36 g; Fiber 2 g;
  T Fat 18 g; 46% Calories from Fat; Chol 84 mg; Sod 241 mg.

Cream Scones

2 cups flour
2 teaspoons baking powder
2 teaspoons sugar
1/2 teaspoon salt

1/4 cup butter
2 eggs
1/2 cup (or more) cream
1 teaspoon water

Mix flour, baking powder, sugar and salt in bowl. Cut in butter until crumbly. Reserve a small amount of egg white to brush tops of scones. Beat remaining eggs in bowl. Add to dry ingredients with cream; mix to form dough. Knead for 30 seconds on floured surface. Pat or roll into rectangle 3/4 inch thick. Cut diagonally into diamonds. Brush with mixture of reserved egg white and water. Place on baking sheet. Sprinkle with additional sugar. Bake at 450 degrees for 15 minutes. May add spices, grated orange or lemon rind, raisins or currants.
Yield: 12 servings.

Approx Per Serving: Cal 161; Prot 3 g; Carbo 17 g; Fiber 1 g;
  T Fat 9 g; 49% Calories from Fat; Chol 59 mg; Sod 192 mg.

Raisin Bran Scones

1½ cups Raisin Bran
½ cup milk
2 cups flour
½ cup packed brown sugar
2 teaspoons baking powder
½ teaspoon salt
½ cup unsalted butter, chilled

2 eggs
1½ teaspoons vanilla extract
⅔ cup coarsely chopped
  walnuts
1 egg white
½ teaspoon water

Butter a 10-inch circle in center of baking sheet. Combine cereal and milk in small bowl. Let stand for several minutes. Mix flour, brown sugar, baking powder and salt in bowl. Cut in butter until crumbly. Stir in eggs and vanilla. Add cereal mixture and walnuts; mix to form sticky dough. Pat into 9-inch circle on buttered baking sheet. Brush with mixture of egg white and water. Cut into 8 wedges with serrated knife. Bake at 375 degrees for 30 to 35 minutes or until wooden pick comes out clean. **Yield: 8 servings.**

Approx Per Serving: Cal 405; Prot 8 g; Carbo 51 g; Fiber 3 g;
  T Fat 20 g; 43% Calories from Fat; Chol 86 mg; Sod 311 mg.

Soda Scones

3 cups flour
¼ cup sugar
½ teaspoon baking soda
2 teaspoons cream of tartar

½ cup butter, softened
¼ cup milk
¼ cup water
2 eggs

Mix flour, sugar, baking soda and cream of tartar in bowl. Cut in butter with pastry cutter until mixture is of consistency of coarse crumbs. Add milk, water and eggs; mix with spatula to form dough. Pat into 8-inch baking pan sprayed with nonstick cooking spray. Bake at 400 degrees for 25 minutes. Serve warm with jam or preserves and whipped cream or Devonshire cream. **Yield: 12 servings.**

Approx Per Serving: Cal 214; Prot 5 g; Carbo 28 g; Fiber 1 g;
  T Fat 9 g; 38% Calories from Fat; Chol 57 mg; Sod 113 mg.

Wenham Town Hall

Appetizers
and Beverages

Antipasto

1 large Bermuda onion, chopped
½ cup olive oil
½ cup vinegar
1 12-ounce bottle of chili sauce
1 14-ounce bottle of catsup
1 6-ounce jar stuffed green
  olives

1 8-ounce jar sweet pickle
  relish
1 8-ounce jar onion relish
2 6-ounce cans water-pack
  tuna, drained

Sauté onion in olive oil in large skillet. Add vinegar, chili sauce and catsup. Bring to a boil, stirring frequently. Cut olives into halves. Combine with pickle relish, onion relish and tuna in bowl; mix well. Pour into hot mixture; mix well. Pour into containers with covers. Chill until serving time. Serve as spread for crackers. May be stored, covered, in refrigerator for 2 weeks. May be frozen. **Yield: 24 servings.**

Approx Per Serving: Cal 127; Prot 5 g; Carbo 15 g; Fiber 1 g;
  T Fat 6 g; 40% Calories from Fat; Chol 8 mg; Sod 727 mg.

Eleanor E. Thompson, Director, Wenham Museum

Cayenne Wafers

1 cup shredded sharp Cheddar
  cheese
¼ cup margarine, softened
¼ cup unsalted butter, softened

1 teaspoon salt
¼ teaspoon (scant) cayenne
  pepper
1 cup flour

Combine cheese, margarine, butter, salt and cayenne pepper in bowl; mix well. Add flour; mix well. Shape into ball. Chill, covered, in refrigerator for 30 minutes. Divide dough into 32 portions; shape each into ball. Place on ungreased baking sheet; flatten. Bake at 350 degrees for 15 minutes or until golden brown. Cool in pan for several minutes. Remove to wire rack to cool completely. May be stored in airtight container for several weeks. **Yield: 32 servings.**

Approx Per Serving: Cal 54; Prot 1 g; Carbo 3 g; Fiber <1 g;
  T Fat 4 g; 68% Calories from Fat; Chol 8 mg; Sod 106 mg.

Wenham Tea House

*Make an **Almond Cheese Ball** of 2 cups shredded Cheddar cheese,
3 ounces cream cheese, ¼ cup chopped pimentos, ¾ cup sliced
almonds, 1 tablespoon lemon juice, 1 teaspoon Worcestershire sauce,
1 teaspoon grated onion, ½ teaspoon salt and cayenne pepper
to taste. Shape into ball and coat with ¼ cup additional almonds.*

Cheese and Tomato Luncheon Sandwiches

3 cups shredded Swiss cheese
2/3 cup chopped tomato
2/3 cup mayonnaise-type salad
  dressing

1/4 cup chopped green onions
1 round loaf unsliced
  pumpernickle bread

Combine first 4 ingredients in bowl; mix well. Slice bread to but not through bottom. Spread cheese mixture on one side of each slice. Wrap in foil; place on baking sheet. Bake at 325 degrees for 15 minutes or until cheese is melted. Cut into servings. Place on serving plate. **Yield: 16 servings.**

Approx Per Serving: Cal 191; Prot 9 g; Carbo 17 g; Fiber 2 g;
  T Fat 10 g; 47% Calories from Fat; Chol 22 mg; Sod 282 mg.

Jane Shute, Tea House Staff

Cocktail Sweet 'n Sour Meatballs

2 pounds ground beef
1 1/2 cups bread crumbs
1/2 cup minced onion
1 tablespoon Worcestershire
  sauce
2 eggs, beaten
1 teaspoon salt

1 teaspoon garlic powder
1 teaspoon pepper
1   14-ounce bottle of catsup
1   12-ounce jar grape jelly
1/2 cup seedless raisins
1 teaspoon lemon juice
1 small onion, chopped

Combine first 8 ingredients in large bowl; mix well. Shape mixture into 1-inch balls. Arrange on greased baking sheet. Bake at 350 degrees for 20 minutes. Place in chafing dish. Combine catsup, grape jelly, raisins, lemon juice and onion in saucepan. Cook over medium heat for 10 minutes, stirring frequently. Pour over meatballs. **Yield: 60 servings.**

Nutritional information for this recipe is not available.

Julie Perkins, Tea House Waitress

Crab Meat Canapés

1/2 cup margarine, softened
1   5-ounce jar Old English
  cheese, softened
1 1/2 teaspoons mayonnaise

1/2 teaspoon garlic salt
1/2 teaspoon seasoned salt
1   6-ounce can crab meat
12 English muffin halves

Mix first 6 ingredients in bowl. Spread on muffin halves; place on baking sheet. Bake at 425 degrees for 15 minutes. **Yield: 12 servings.**

Approx Per Serving: Cal 195; Prot 8 g; Carbo 14 g; Fiber 1 g;
  T Fat 12 g; 55% Calories from Fat; Chol 20 mg; Sod 608 mg.

Wenham Tea House

Cuke-a-Dillies

1/4 cup mayonnaise
16 ounces cream cheese,
  softened
1/2 envelope Italian salad
  dressing mix

1 loaf party rye bread
2 cucumbers, thinly sliced
Dillweed to taste

Blend mayonnaise and cream cheese in bowl. Mix in dressing mix. Spread on bread slices; top each with 1 slice cucumber. Sprinkle with dillweed. Place on serving plate. **Yield: 40 servings.**

Approx Per Serving: Cal 66; Prot 1 g; Carbo 4 g; Fiber 1 g;
  T Fat 5 g; 70% Calories from Fat; Chol 13 mg; Sod 93 mg.

Dodie Welch, Wenham Exchange

Hanky-Pankies

1 pound hot Italian sausage
1 pound ground beef
1 pound Velveeta cheese,
  chopped

1/8 teaspoon salt
1/2 teaspoon garlic powder
1/2 teaspoon oregano
2 loaves party rye bread

Remove casing from sausage. Brown sausage and ground beef in skillet, stirring until crumbly; drain. Add cheese. Cook until cheese melts, stirring frequently. Add seasonings. Spread by tablespoonfuls onto bread slices; place on baking sheet. Bake at 350 degrees for 8 to 10 minutes or until edges of bread are brown. Place on serving dish. May freeze unbaked slices on covered tray until firm. Store in airtight container in freezer until needed. **Yield: 40 servings.**

Approx Per Serving: Cal 115; Prot 7 g; Carbo 6 g; Fiber 1 g;
  T Fat 7 g; 57% Calories from Fat; Chol 23 mg; Sod 324 mg.

Patricia Blanchard, Tea House Waitress

Scallop and Bacon Wraps

12 scallops

6 slices bacon, cut into halves

Wrap scallop in bacon half; secure with wooden pick. Place on rack in baking pan. Bake at 425 degrees for 15 minutes or until bacon is brown and crisp. May substitute chicken livers for scallops. **Yield: 12 servings.**

Approx Per Serving: Cal 25; Prot 2 g; Carbo <1 g; Fiber 0 g;
  T Fat 2 g; 60% Calories from Fat; Chol 5 mg; Sod 62 mg.

Wenham Tea House

Iced Scallop Salad

1 pound bay scallops
Juice of 1 lime
1/4 cup watercress leaves
1/2 cup mayonnaise
2 tablespoons chopped parsley

2 tablespoons chopped green
  onions
1 teaspoon fresh chopped dill
2 teaspoons lime juice

Steam scallops over water in steamer until tender. Do not overcook. Place in bowl of ice water to stop cooking. Combine scallops and juice of 1 lime in bowl; toss to mix. Chill, covered, in refrigerator. Combine watercress leaves, mayonnaise, parsley, green onions, dill and 2 teaspoons lime juice in blender container. Process until puréed. Arrange scallops on serving dish lined with mixed greens. Drizzle with green sauce. **Yield: 6 servings.**

Approx Per Serving: Cal 203; Prot 14 g; Carbo 3 g; Fiber <1 g;
    T Fat 15 g; 66% Calories from Fat; Chol 37 mg; Sod 225 mg.

Mary Heath Tully, Patron

Hot Spinach Hors d'Oeuvres

2 10-ounce packages frozen
   chopped spinach
2 cups seasoned herb stuffing
   mix
4 eggs, beaten

1/2 cup melted butter
1 clove of garlic, minced
1 cup grated Parmesan cheese
1/2 teaspoon thyme
Pepper to taste

Cook spinach using package directions; drain well. Combine spinach, stuffing mix, eggs, butter, garlic, Parmesan cheese, thyme and pepper in bowl; mix well. Chill, covered, for 2 hours or longer. Shape into 1-inch balls. Place on baking sheet. Bake at 300 degrees for 30 minutes or until golden brown. Place on serving dish. May freeze, covered, on baking sheet until firm. Store in airtight container in freezer until needed. **Yield: 35 servings.**

Approx Per Serving: Cal 62; Prot 3 g; Carbo 4 g; Fiber <1 g;
    T Fat 4 g; 58% Calories from Fat; Chol 33 mg; Sod 140 mg.

Joanne Maestranzi, Board of Directors, WVIS

*For **Stuffed Mushrooms**, chop the stems of 1 pound of mushrooms
and mix with 1 minced onion, 2 tablespoons butter, 1 tablespoon oil,
1/4 cup dry bread crumbs, 1/3 cup grated Parmesan cheese and 1/4
teaspoon tarragon. Brush mushroom caps with butter, fill with
bread crumb mixture and bake at 350 degrees for 10 to 15 minutes.*

Veggie Bars

2 8-count cans crescent rolls
16 ounces cream cheese,
   softened
1 cup mayonnaise

1 envelope ranch salad
   dressing mix
2 cups mixed chopped carrots,
   broccoli, onions, mushrooms
   and black olives

Unroll crescent roll dough. Separate into rectangles. Spread on baking pan, sealing perforations. Bake at 300 degrees for 7 to 10 minutes or until brown. Cool to room temperature. Combine cream cheese, mayonnaise and dressing mix in bowl; mix well. Spread cream cheese mixture over crust. Sprinkle with mixed vegetables, pressing lightly into cream cheese layer. Chill, covered, until serving time. Cut into servings; place on serving dish. **Yield: 36 servings.**

Approx Per Serving: Cal 139; Prot 2 g; Carbo 6 g; Fiber <1 g;
   T Fat 12 g; 77% Calories from Fat; Chol 17 mg; Sod 243 mg.

Mrs. Spiri, WVIS Friend

Cheesy Zucchini Squares

1 cup Bisquick baking mix
1/2 cup chopped onion
1 1/2 teaspoons chopped parsley
1/2 cup melted butter
4 eggs, beaten

Pepper to taste
2 cups sharp Cheddar cheese
1 12-inch zucchini, thinly
   sliced

Combine Bisquick, onion and parsley in bowl; mix well. Add butter and eggs; mix well. Add pepper and cheese; mix well. Stir in zucchini. Spoon into ungreased 9x13-inch baking dish. Bake at 350 degrees for 30 to 35 minutes or until brown. Cut into servings. Serve warm or cold. **Yield: 50 servings.**

Approx Per Serving: Cal 53; Prot 2 g; Carbo 2 g; Fiber <1 g;
   T Fat 4 g; 70% Calories from Fat; Chol 27 mg; Sod 81 mg.

Wenham Tea House

*For low-fat dips, try unsweetened applesauce or a mixture of
equal parts yogurt and cottage cheese processed in the
blender and seasoned with herbs or spices.*

Boursin-Style Cheese

8 ounces cream cheese, softened
1/4 cup butter, softened
1/2 teaspoon Beau Monde
  seasoning
1 clove of garlic, minced
1 teaspoon water

1/4 teaspoon Worcestershire
  sauce
1 teaspoon minced fresh parsley
1/4 teaspoon vinegar
1/4 teaspoon Herbs of Provence

Beat cream cheese and butter in mixer bowl beat until smooth and fluffy. Add remaining ingredients; mix well. Spoon into small serving bowl. Serve with assorted crackers. **Herbs of Provence:** Mix 3 tablespoons marjoram, 3 tablespoons summer savory, 1 1/2 teaspoons rosemary, 1/2 teaspoon fennel, 3 tablespoons thyme, 1 tablespoon basil and 1/2 teaspoon sage together. Store in airtight container. **Yield: 20 (1-tablespoon) servings.**

Approx Per Serving: Cal 60; Prot 1 g; Carbo <1 g; Fiber <1 g;
  T Fat 6 g; 92% Calories from Fat; Chol 19 mg; Sod 54 mg.

Hope C. Ayers, WVIS Member

Gwenn Spread

1 15-ounce can Mezzetta
  roasted red peppers
1 clove of garlic, minced
1/4 cup olive oil
1 teaspoon cumin
1/2 teaspoon roasted red pepper
  flakes

1 teaspoon paprika
6 6-inch rounds Boboli bread
18 tablespoons (or more) olive
  oil
Freshly ground black pepper to
  taste
3 4-inch rolls Cheve cheese

Process red peppers and garlic in blender until almost smooth. Heat pepper mixture in 1/4 cup olive oil in skillet. Add cumin, red pepper flakes and paprika. Cook over low heat for 5 minutes, stirring frequently. Let stand for several hours to enhance flavor. Place bread rounds on baking sheet. Top each with 3 tablespoons (or more) olive oil. Sprinkle generously with black pepper. Bake at 375 degrees for 15 to 20 minutes or until brown. Cut into small irregularly shaped serving-size pieces. Reheat sauce to serving temperature. Slice Cheve cheese into 1/2-inch rounds. Arrange in center of large serving dish. Pour hot sauce over cheese. Surround with bread pieces. **Yield: 12 servings.**

Approx Per Serving: Cal 399; Prot 11 g; Carbo 3 g; Fiber 1 g;
  T Fat 39 g; 87% Calories from Fat; Chol 45 mg; Sod 265 mg.
  Nutritional information does not include Boboli bread.

Gwen Cohen, Patron

Lobster Pâté

8 ounces cream cheese, softened
1/4 cup white wine
1/4 teaspoon onion salt
1/2 teaspoon seasoned salt

1/2 teaspoon dried dill
1 1/2 cups chopped cooked
   lobster

Combine cream cheese, wine, onion salt, seasoned salt and dill in bowl; mix well. Add lobster; mix well. Chill until serving time. Serve with assorted crackers. **Yield: 10 servings.**

Approx Per Serving: Cal 105; Prot 6 g; Carbo 1 g; Fiber 0 g;
   T Fat 8 g; 72% Calories from Fat; Chol 40 mg; Sod 266 mg.

Margaret McNamara, Past President, WVIS

Easy and Tasty Hors d'Oeuvres

8 ounces cream cheese

1   8-ounce jar hot pepper jelly

Place cream cheese on serving dish. Spoon jelly onto top of cheese. Serve with crackers. **Yield: 12 servings.**

Approx Per Serving: Cal 117; Prot 1 g; Carbo 14 g; Fiber <1 g;
   T Fat 7 g; 49% Calories from Fat; Chol 21 mg; Sod 60 mg.

Wenham Tea House

Wagon Wheel Dip

1/2 cup chopped sweet pickles
1/2 cup chopped pimento-
   stuffed olives
1 small onion, chopped
1 small green bell pepper,
   chopped

1 clove of garlic, minced
8 ounces cream cheese, softened
1 tablespoon whipping cream
1/2 cup mayonnaise
1/4 cup catsup

Combine pickles, olives, onion, green pepper and garlic in bowl; mix well. Drain. Combine cream cheese and cream in bowl; mix well. Add mayonnaise and catsup; beat well. Stir in drained mixture. Chill, covered, until serving time. Serve with large corn chips or veggies for dipping. May substitute milk for whipping cream. **Yield: 16 servings.**

Approx Per Serving: Cal 126; Prot 1 g; Carbo 5 g; Fiber 1 g;
   T Fat 12 g; 80% Calories from Fat; Chol 21 mg; Sod 304 mg.

Marilyn Corning, Wenham Museum Staff

Golden Punch

2 20-ounce cans juice-pack
   crushed pineapple
2 6-ounce cans frozen
   lemonade concentrate, thawed

¹/₄ cup sugar
1 28-ounce bottle of club soda,
   chilled
1 tray ice cubes

Process undrained pineapple 1 can at a time in blender for 15 to 20 seconds or until thick. Combine pineapple, lemonade concentrate and sugar in chilled punch bowl; mix well. Stir in club soda. Add ice cubes just before serving. May make Champagne punch by adding 1 bottle of Champagne with club soda. **Yield: 10 (1-cup) servings.**

Approx Per Serving: Cal 149; Prot 1 g; Carbo 39 g; Fiber 1 g;
   T Fat <1 g; 1% Calories from Fat; Chol 0 mg; Sod 20 mg.

Wenham Tea House

Strawberry-Lemonade Mix

1 pint fresh strawberries
1¹/₄ cups fresh lemon juice

2¹/₂ cups (or less) sugar

Crush strawberries in bowl. Add lemon juice and sugar; mix until sugar is dissolved. Store in covered jar in refrigerator. Stir ¹/₄ cup mix into ³/₄ cup water or club soda for each serving. **Yield: 18 (¹/₄-cup) servings.**

Approx Per Serving: Cal 116; Prot <1 g; Carbo 30 g; Fiber <1 g;
   T Fat <1 g; 1% Calories from Fat; Chol 0 mg; Sod 1 mg.

Gail S. Clemenzi, Board of Directors, WVIS

Sparkling Strawberry Punch

2 10-ounce packages frozen
   sweetened strawberries,
   partially thawed
1 6-ounce can frozen
   lemonade concentrate,
   partially thawed
1¹/₄ quarts rosé, chilled

2 28-ounce bottles of ginger
   ale, chilled
1 28-ounce bottle of club soda,
   chilled
¹/₄ cup sugar
2 trays ice cubes
Sections of 1 orange

Combine strawberries and lemonade concentrate in blender container. Process until well blended. Mix strawberry mixture with next 4 ingredients in chilled punch bowl until sugar is completely dissolved. Add ice cubes. Garnish with orange sections. **Yield: 30 (¹/₂-cup) servings.**

Approx Per Serving: Cal 84; Prot <1 g; Carbo 15 g; Fiber 1 g;
   T Fat <1 g; 0% Calories from Fat; Chol 0 mg; Sod 12 mg.

Wenham Tea House

Six-Fruit Punch for Forty

1 cup sugar
1 cup water
2 10-ounce packages frozen
  strawberries
1 24-ounce can cranberry juice
  cocktail, chilled
1 quart orange juice, chilled

1 24-ounce can pineapple
  juice, chilled
1 cup lemon juice
1 24-ounce can pink
  grapefruit juice, chilled
4 quarts ginger ale, chilled

Combine sugar and water in saucepan. Heat over low heat until sugar is dissolved, stirring constantly. Add strawberries, stirring until thawed. Combine strawberry mixture with next 5 ingredients in punch bowl; mix well. Add ginger ale just before serving. **Yield: 40 (6-ounce) servings.**

Approx Per Serving: Cal 97; Prot <1 g; Carbo 25 g; Fiber 1 g;
  T Fat <1 g; 1% Calories from Fat; Chol 0 mg; Sod 8 mg.

Wenham Tea House

Wine Punch

2 bottles each of Sangria and
  sparkling Burgundy, chilled

1 quart ginger ale, chilled
1 quart raspberry sherbet

Combine wines and ginger ale in punch bowl; stir gently to mix. Add sherbet. Serve immediately. **Yield: 20 servings.**

Approx Per Serving: Cal 174; Prot 1 g; Carbo 19 g; Fiber 0 g;
  T Fat 1 g; 4% Calories from Fat; Chol 3 mg; Sod 29 mg.

Wenham Tea House

Hot Cranberry Delight

2 tablespoons whole cloves
1 tablespoon whole allspice
1 1/2-inch cinnamon stick,
  broken
1/2 cup (or more) sugar

1/4 teaspoon salt
5 cups water
2 1/2 cups grapefruit juice
2 16-ounce cans cranberry sauce
Red food coloring

Tie cloves, allspice and cinnamon stick in cheesecloth. Combine sugar, salt and water in large saucepan; mix well. Add grapefruit juice, cranberry sauce and spices. Bring to a boil, stirring frequently. Reduce heat. Simmer, covered, for 5 minutes. Remove spices. Add several drops of food coloring; mix well. **Yield: 12 servings.**

Approx Per Serving: Cal 170; Prot <1 g; Carbo 44 g; Fiber 2 g;
  T Fat <1 g; 1% Calories from Fat; Chol 0 mg; Sod 68 mg.

Wenham Tea House

Bessie Buker School

Soups

Blueberry Soup

2 cups fresh blueberries
4 cups hot water
1 cup sugar

1/2 lemon, thinly sliced
1/2 cinnamon stick
2 cups sour cream

Place blueberries in saucepan with hot water to cover. Add sugar, lemon slices and cinnamon. Bring to a boil; reduce heat. Simmer for 20 minutes, stirring occasionally. Strain through colander lined with cheesecloth into bowl; cool. Chill in refrigerator. Reserve 6 tablespoons sour cream. Stir remaining sour cream into soup before serving. Place dollop of reserved sour cream on each serving. **Yield: 6 servings.**

Approx Per Serving: Cal 321; Prot 3 g; Carbo 44 g; Fiber 1 g;
    T Fat 16 g; 44% Calories from Fat; Chol 34 mg; Sod 45 mg.

Wenham Tea House

Cucumber Soup

1 cucumber, peeled, sliced
1 cup chicken broth
3/4 cup cottage cheese
Dill to taste

1 cup evaporated milk
1 cup light cream
Salt and white pepper to taste

Purée all ingredients in blender. Chill before serving. **Yield: 4 servings.**

Approx Per Serving: Cal 320; Prot 12 g; Carbo 12 g; Fiber 1 g;
    T Fat 26 g; 71% Calories from Fat; Chol 91 mg; Sod 442 mg.

Wenham Tea House

Gazpacho Soup

4 cups tomato juice
2 beef bouillon cubes
2 tomatoes, peeled, seeded,
    chopped
1/2 cup chopped unpeeled
    cucumber
1/4 cup chopped onion

1/4 cup chopped green bell
    pepper
1/4 cup wine vinegar
2 tablespoons oil
1 teaspoon salt
1 teaspoon Worcestershire sauce
3 drops of Tabasco sauce

Bring tomato juice to a boil in saucepan. Add bouillon cubes, stirring until dissolved. Remove from heat; cool. Add tomatoes and remaining ingredients; mix well. Chill until serving time. Serve in chilled bowls. **Yield: 6 servings.**

Approx Per Serving: Cal 86; Prot 2 g; Carbo 11 g; Fiber 2 g;
    T Fat 5 g; 45% Calories from Fat; Chol 0 mg; Sod 1243 mg.

Wenham Tea House

Chilled Raspberry-Lime Rickey Soup

24 ounces frozen raspberries,
  partially thawed
1/4 cup pineapple juice

3/4 cup lime juice
2 cups 7-Up
1/2 cup gin

Combine raspberries, pineapple juice, lime juice, 7-Up and gin in blender container. Process until smooth. Pour into champagne glasses. Garnish with lime sherbet. Serve immediately. **Yield: 6 servings.**

Approx Per Serving: Cal 205; Prot 1 g; Carbo 42 g; Fiber 5 g;
  T Fat <1 g; 1% Calories from Fat; Chol 0 mg; Sod 11 mg.

Wenham Tea House

Cold Strawberry Soup

2 cups strawberries
1 cup water
1/2 cup sugar

1 cup wine
2 teaspoons lemon juice

Combine strawberries, water and sugar in blender container. Process until puréed. Stir in wine and lemon juice. Chill in refrigerator before serving. Garnish with dollop of sour cream. **Yield: 4 servings.**

Approx Per Serving: Cal 159; Prot 1 g; Carbo 31 g; Fiber 2 g;
  T Fat <1 g; 2% Calories from Fat; Chol 0 mg; Sod 4 mg.

Wenham Tea House

Tomato Mist

1   46-ounce can tomato juice
1/4 cup lemon juice
1 teaspoon sugar
2 teaspoons Worcestershire
  sauce

1/4 teaspoon onion powder
2 teaspoons prepared
  horseradish
Salt to taste

Combine tomato juice, lemon juice, sugar, Worcestershire sauce, onion powder, horseradish and salt in bowl; mix well. Chill in refrigerator before serving. Garnish with lemon. **Yield: 10 servings.**

Approx Per Serving: Cal 27; Prot 1 g; Carbo 7 g; Fiber 1 g;
  T Fat <1 g; 3% Calories from Fat; Chol 0 mg; Sod 482 mg.

Wenham Tea House

Cold Vegetable Soup

4 cups canned tomatoes
1 12-ounce can vegetable juice cocktail
2 cups tomato juice
1 cucumber, peeled, chopped
1 green bell pepper, chopped

2 stalks celery, chopped
2 to 3 scallions, chopped
1 tablespoon sugar
Pepper, parsley and chives to taste

Process all ingredients in blender until smooth. Chill in refrigerator before serving. **Yield: 8 servings.**

Approx Per Serving: Cal 58; Prot 2 g; Carbo 13 g; Fiber 3 g;
T Fat <1 g; 6% Calories from Fat; Chol 0 mg; Sod 580 mg.

Wenham Tea House

Christmas Soup

1 6-ounce can frozen orange juice concentrate, thawed

1 46-ounce can tomato juice
1 slice onion

Combine all ingredients in saucepan. Cook over low heat until heated through, stirring gently. Do not boil. Pour into soup cups. Garnish with dollop of whipped cream and parsley sprig. **Yield: 6 servings.**

Approx Per Serving: Cal 83; Prot 2 g; Carbo 20 g; Fiber 2 g;
T Fat <1 g; 2% Calories from Fat; Chol 0 mg; Sod 786 mg.

Dru Farley, Exchange Book Shop

Mock Turtle Soup

2¹/₂ quarts water
1¹/₂ pounds lean ground beef
1 14-ounce bottle of catsup
6¹/₂ tablespoons Worcestershire sauce
5 tablespoons lemon juice

20 gingersnaps
6 large carrots
6 stalks celery
10 ounces mushrooms, sliced
5 hard-boiled eggs, chopped

Bring water to a boil in large saucepan. Add ground beef in small portions. Stir in catsup, Worcestershire sauce and lemon juice. Put gingersnaps, carrots and celery through food grinder. Stir into ground beef mixture gradually. Add mushrooms. Simmer for 1 hour or until of desired consistency, stirring occasionally. Ladle into serving bowls. Top with chopped eggs. **Yield: 18 servings.**

Approx Per Serving: Cal 177; Prot 10 g; Carbo 17 g; Fiber 2 g;
T Fat 8 g; 39% Calories from Fat; Chol 84 mg; Sod 388 mg.

Robert H. Bode, WVIS Friend

Cream of Mushroom Soup

8 ounces mushrooms
2 tablespoons margarine
1 onion, chopped
2 tablespoons margarine
1/4 cup flour

1 teaspoon salt
1/4 teaspoon white pepper
1 10-ounce can chicken broth
1 broth can water
1 cup half and half

Slice enough mushrooms to measure 1 cup; chop remaining mushrooms. Sauté sliced mushrooms in 2 tablespoons margarine in saucepan until golden brown; remove to platter with slotted spoon. Sauté chopped mushrooms and onion in remaining 2 tablespoons margarine until onion is tender. Add flour, salt and white pepper, stirring well. Cook over low heat for 1 minute, stirring constantly. Remove from heat. Add chicken broth and water. Bring to a boil, stirring constantly. Cook for 1 minute, stirring constantly. Stir in half and half and sliced mushrooms. Ladle into serving bowls. Garnish with parsley. **Yield: 6 servings.**

Approx Per Serving: Cal 165; Prot 4 g; Carbo 10 g; Fiber 1 g;
  T Fat 13 g; 68% Calories from Fat; Chol 15 mg; Sod 613 mg.

Meredith Poor, Hobbs House Staff

Carrot Soup

2 onions, chopped
2 stalks celery, chopped
1 1/2 pounds carrots, peeled, sliced
3 tablespoons butter
Salt and pepper to taste

2 teaspoons dried dill or 2
  tablespoons minced fresh
  dill (optional)
2 quarts chicken broth
Nutmeg to taste

Sauté onions, celery and carrots in butter in saucepan over medium-low heat for 10 minutes. Add salt, pepper, dill and chicken broth. Simmer, covered, for 45 minutes. Purée in food mill or food processor; return to saucepan. Heat to serving temperature over low heat; do not boil. Season with nutmeg. **Yield: 10 servings.**

Variations:

1. Substitute 1 quart cider or apple juice for 1 quart chicken broth.
2. Add 1 1/2 cups chopped apples halfway through simmering time.
3. Sauté one or two cloves of garlic with vegetables.
4. Blend 2 cups cream with puréed mixture for a richer soup. Be sure to adjust seasonings.

Approx Per Serving: Cal 104; Prot 5 g; Carbo 10 g; Fiber 3 g;
  T Fat 5 g; 41% Calories from Fat; Chol 10 mg; Sod 681 mg.
  Nutritional information is for basic recipe only.

Michael Mockler, Head Cook, Wenham Tea House

French Onion Soup

4 to 6 large red onions, thinly
  sliced
4 to 6 tablespoons butter
1/4 to 1/2 cup sugar
Salt to taste
1/2 teaspoon pepper

6 cups beef stock
2 to 4 tablespoons ruby port
6 thick slices French bread,
  toasted
1 cup shredded Gruyère cheese

Sauté onions in butter over medium-low heat in large saucepan for 20 minutes or until tender. Sprinkle with sugar, tossing to coat. Cook for 10 minutes longer or until caramelized. Add salt, pepper, beef stock and port; mix well. Simmer for 30 to 40 minutes, stirring occasionally. Pour into ovenproof soup bowls. Top each serving with slice of French bread; sprinkle with cheese. Place bowls under broiler. Broil until cheese is melted and bubbly. **Yield: 6 servings.**

Approx Per Serving: Cal 426; Prot 14 g; Carbo 47 g; Fiber 3 g; T Fat 20 g; 43% Calories from Fat; Chol 52 mg; Sod 1149 mg.

Joyce Thibault, Second Cook, Wenham Tea House

Seafood Chowder

1/2 cup minced onion
1/4 cup butter
2 cups fish stock
1/2 cup white wine
1/2 cup thinly sliced celery
1 cup thinly sliced carrot
1 cup chopped potato
1 bay leaf
1/2 teaspoon thyme
2 teaspoons salt

Pepper to taste
1 pound haddock, cut into
  small pieces
1 cup milk
1/2 cup flour
2 cups milk
1 cup half and half
6 ounces flaked crab meat
Parsley to taste

Sauté onion in butter in saucepan until tender. Add fish stock, wine, celery, carrot, potato, bay leaf, thyme, salt, pepper and haddock. Simmer for 20 minutes, stirring occasionally. Remove bay leaf. Whisk 1 cup milk and flour together in bowl until thin paste forms. Add to chowder slowly. Cook until thickened, stirring frequently. Add remaining 2 cups milk, half and half, crab meat and parsley slowly. Cook until heated through, stirring frequently. **Yield: 8 servings.**

Approx Per Serving: Cal 295; Prot 23 g; Carbo 18 g; Fiber 1 g; T Fat 14 g; 43% Calories from Fat; Chol 94 mg; Sod 936 mg.

Wenham Tea House

Spinach Soup

3 pounds fresh spinach, trimmed	2 cups chicken stock
1½ cups finely chopped onions	2 cups low-fat milk
¼ cup unsalted butter	Salt, pepper and nutmeg to taste

Wash spinach; do not drain. Place spinach in large saucepan. Cook, covered, over high heat until spinach is wilted. Drain, reserving liquid; set aside. Sauté onions in butter in skillet until tender and golden. Combine onions and spinach in food processor container. Process until puréed. Combine with chicken stock, milk and reserved spinach liquid in saucepan. Simmer slowly, stirring frequently. Stir in salt, pepper and nutmeg. Ladle into serving bowls. Garnish with thin slices of lemon and chopped chives. **Yield: 6 servings.**

Approx Per Serving: Cal 184; Prot 11 g; Carbo 15 g; Fiber 8 g;
    T Fat 11 g; 47% Calories from Fat; Chol 28 mg; Sod 543 mg.

Wenham Tea House

Squash Soup

2 butternut squash, peeled, cubed	3 tablespoons butter
2 onions, chopped	2 quarts chicken broth
2 stalks celery, chopped	Salt and pepper to taste
2 carrots, chopped	Nutmeg to taste

Cook squash in a small amount of water in saucepan until tender. Drain and set aside. Sauté onions, celery and carrots in butter in saucepan over medium-low heat for 10 minutes. Add broth, salt and pepper; mix well. Simmer, covered, for 30 minutes. Add squash. Pour mixture into food processor container. Process until smooth. Return to saucepan; add nutmeg. Cook until heated through. Do not boil. May add 2 cups cream for richer soup. May substitute 1 quart apple juice or apple cider for chicken broth and add 1½ cups chopped apples halfway through cooking process. May substitute 3 cans pumpkin for squash. **Yield: 12 servings.**

Approx Per Serving: Cal 122; Prot 5 g; Carbo 18 g; Fiber 5 g;
    T Fat 4 g; 28% Calories from Fat; Chol 8 mg; Sod 557 mg.

Michael Mockler, Head Cook, Wenham Tea House

*Make **Cold Spinach Soup** with 3 packages of frozen chopped spinach cooked in 1 cup chicken broth. Purée and add 2 cups cream, 1½ teaspoons nutmeg, ½ teaspoon Krazy salt, ½ teaspoon chervil, ½ teaspoon salt and ½ teaspoon pepper. Add cherry tomatoes and chill for 3 hours.*

Tomato Toddy

1 10-ounce can tomato soup
1 10-ounce can beef broth
1 soup can water

¹/₄ teaspoon marjoram
¹/₄ teaspoon thyme

Mix all ingredients in saucepan. Simmer until heated through, stirring occasionally. Ladle into serving bowls. Garnish with croutons. **Yield: 4 servings.**

Approx Per Serving: Cal 53; Prot 2 g; Carbo 9 g; Fiber <1 g;
    T Fat 1 g; 20% Calories from Fat; Chol <1 mg; Sod 723 mg.

Wenham Tea House

Tomato-Zucchini Soup

1 zucchini, finely chopped
¹/₂ cup chopped onion
1 tablespoon olive oil
1 large tomato, chopped
¹/₄ teaspoon oregano

1 cup tomato juice
1 cup chicken broth
1 tablespoon tomato paste
Salt and pepper to taste
1 tablespoon minced fresh basil

Sauté zucchini and onion in olive oil in saucepan for 5 to 10 minutes or until onion is tender. Add tomato and next 6 ingredients; mix well. Simmer for 15 minutes or until vegetables are tender. Stir in basil just before serving. **Yield: 4 servings.**

Approx Per Serving: Cal 76; Prot 3 g; Carbo 8 g; Fiber 2 g;
    T Fat 4 g; 44% Calories from Fat; Chol <1 mg; Sod 421 mg.

Cyndy Morong, Tea House Waitress

Summer Harvest Soup

2 to 3 onions, chopped
2 to 3 cloves of garlic, chopped
3 tablespoons olive oil
Potatoes, quartered
Tomatoes, peeled, quartered
Green beans, chopped
Carrots, chopped

Cabbage, shredded
Cucumbers, chopped
Radishes, sliced
Kale, thinly sliced
Beets, peeled, cooked, cubed
Chicken broth

Sauté onions and garlic in olive oil in 6-quart stockpot until tender. Add next 9 ingredients. Stir in enough chicken broth to cover. Simmer for 1 hour or until vegetables are tender. Purée a small amount at a time in food processor. Return to stockpot. Cook until heated through. **Yield: variable.**

Nutritional information for this recipe is not available.

Susanne (Snooky) Phippen, Past President, WVIS

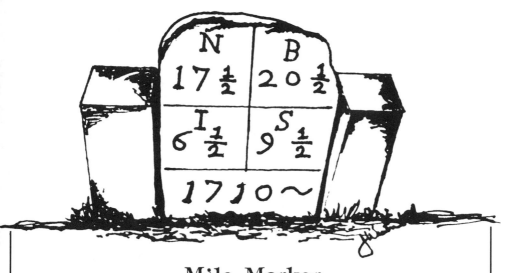

Mile Marker
Wenham Town Hall

Salads

Cherry-Wine Jellied Salad

1 21-ounce can dark red
   cherries
1 cup water
1 6-ounce package cherry
   gelatin

1 cup dry red wine
1 cup chopped walnuts

Drain cherries, reserving juice in saucepan. Add 1 cup water to reserved juice. Bring to a boil. Pour over cherry gelatin in bowl, stirring until dissolved. Add wine; mix well. Chill in refrigerator until partially set. Add cherries and walnuts; mix well. Pour into mold. Chill until set. Unmold onto salad plate. **Yield: 8 servings.**

Approx Per Serving: Cal 258; Prot 5 g; Carbo 38 g; Fiber 1 g;
    T Fat 9 g; 33% Calories from Fat; Chol 0 mg; Sod 73 mg.

Shirley Ernst, Wenham Exchange

Fruit Ambrosia

1 16-ounce can fruit cocktail,
   drained
1 16-ounce can green grapes,
   drained
1 11-ounce can mandarin
   oranges, drained

1 16-ounce can pineapple
   tidbits, drained
1 cup miniature marshmallows
1 cup coconut
1 cup sour cream

Combine fruit cocktail, grapes, mandarin oranges, pineapple, marshmallows and coconut in bowl; mix well. Fold in sour cream. Spoon into serving dish. Chill until serving time. Garnish with additional coconut. **Yield: 10 servings.**

Approx Per Serving: Cal 192; Prot 2 g; Carbo 33 g; Fiber 2 g;
    T Fat 7 g; 33% Calories from Fat; Chol 10 mg; Sod 27 mg.

Wenham Tea House

Fruit Compote

1   16-ounce can sliced peaches
1   16-ounce can sliced pears
1   16-ounce can pineapple
    chunks
1   8-ounce can whole cranberry
    sauce

2 cups whipping cream,
    whipped
1/2 cup mayonnaise
3/4 cup confectioners' sugar
1/2 teaspoon vanilla extract
1/4 teaspoon lemon juice

Drain fruit well, reserving juices. Combine fruit juices and cranberry sauce in mixer bowl; mix well. Add fruit, stirring to mix. Chill, covered, in refrigerator overnight. Combine whipped cream, mayonnaise, confectioners' sugar, vanilla and lemon juice in bowl; mix well. Serve as sauce with fruit. **Yield: 8 servings.**

Approx Per Serving: Cal 562; Prot 2 g; Carbo 69 g; Fiber 3 g;
    T Fat 33 g; 51% Calories from Fat; Chol 90 mg; Sod 124 mg.

Wenham Tea House

Solving's Gelatin Mold

2 cups apricot nectar
1   3-ounce package orange
    gelatin
1   3-ounce package lemon
    gelatin
1³/4 cups boiling water

8 ounces cream cheese, softened
1   3-ounce package lime gelatin
1¹/2 cups boiling water
1   8-ounce can crushed
    pineapple, drained

Bring apricot nectar to a boil in saucepan. Add orange gelatin, stirring until dissolved. Pour into gelatin mold. Chill until set. Dissolve lemon gelatin in 1³/4 cups boiling water in bowl. Add cream cheese, stirring until melted. Chill until partially congealed. Pour over congealed orange layer. Dissolve lime gelatin in 1¹/2 cups boiling water in bowl. Chill until partially congealed. Stir in crushed pineapple. Layer over congealed lemon gelatin. Chill until set. Unmold onto salad plate. **Yield: 8 servings.**

Approx Per Serving: Cal 267; Prot 5 g; Carbo 42 g; Fiber 1 g;
    T Fat 10 g; 32% Calories from Fat; Chol 31 mg; Sod 187 mg.

Dorothy Pierce, Retired Tea House Manager

Bacon and Egg and Rice Salad

1 cup uncooked long grain rice
1/4 cup bacon drippings
1/3 cup sugar
1/3 cup vinegar
2 tablespoons water
1 large green bell pepper,
    coarsely chopped
1 large onion, coarsely chopped

2 tablespoons pimento,
    coarsely chopped
1 teaspoon celery seed
1/2 teaspoon salt
Seasoned salt to taste
1/2 teaspoon garlic salt
8 to 12 slices crisp-fried bacon
1 hard-boiled egg, chopped

Cook rice using package directions. Combine bacon drippings, cooked rice, sugar, vinegar, water, green pepper, onion, pimento, celery seed and salts in saucepan. Cook over medium heat until all liquid is absorbed, stirring constantly. Crumble half the bacon into mixture; mix well. Spoon into serving dish. Garnish with remaining bacon slices and chopped egg. May serve hot or chilled. **Yield: 6 servings.**

Approx Per Serving: Cal 340; Prot 7 g; Carbo 40 g; Fiber 1 g;
    T Fat 17 g; 45% Calories from Fat; Chol 102 mg; Sod 657 mg.

Wenham Tea House

Ham Mousse

1 tablespoon unflavored gelatin
1/4 cup cold water
2 cups ground cooked ham
1/2 cup finely minced celery

1 tablespoon minced parsley
2 tablespoons prepared
    horseradish
1 cup whipping cream, whipped

Soften gelatin in cold water in double boiler for 5 minutes. Heat over boiling water until dissolved, stirring constantly. Remove from heat. Stir in ham, celery, parsley and horseradish. Fold in whipped cream. Spoon into ring mold. Chill in refrigerator until set. Unmold onto serving plate. May spoon Waldorf salad in center. **Yield: 12 servings.**

Approx Per Serving: Cal 109; Prot 7 g; Carbo 1 g; Fiber <1 g;
    T Fat 9 g; 71% Calories from Fat; Chol 40 mg; Sod 324 mg.

Wenham Tea House

*Make a delicious salad dressing by melting 1 package
of cream cheese with a small jar of guava jelly and
adding 1 1/2 tablespoons mayonnaise.*

Chicken Mousse

1 tablespoon unflavored gelatin
2 tablespoons cold water
3 egg yolks, beaten
1½ cups chicken broth
1 teaspoon salt
2 cups chopped cooked chicken

½ cup blanched almonds
2 tablespoons finely chopped
  pimento
½ cup whipping cream,
  whipped

Soften gelatin in cold water in bowl for 15 minutes. Combine egg yolks and chicken broth in double boiler. Cook over hot water until mixture coats a spoon, stirring frequently. Stir in gelatin until dissolved. Add salt; mix well. Pour into bowl. Chill until partially congealed. Add chicken, almonds, pimento and whipped cream; mix well. Pour into oiled mold. Chill until set. Unmold onto lettuce-lined serving plate. Garnish with tomatoes and apricots sprinkled with pistachio nuts. **Yield: 8 servings.**

Approx Per Serving: Cal 206; Prot 15 g; Carbo 2 g; Fiber 1 g;
  T Fat 15 g; 66% Calories from Fat; Chol 132 mg; Sod 452 mg.

Wenham Tea House

Crab Meat Salad

8 ounces uncooked macaroni
3 6-ounce cans crab meat
1 carrot, finely chopped
1 medium cucumber, finely
  chopped
¼ to ½ cup finely chopped
  onion

1 green bell pepper, chopped
3 or 4 sweet pickles, chopped
½ cup French dressing
1 cup sour cream
1½ cups mayonnaise
Salt and pepper to taste

Cook macaroni using package directions; drain. Rinse in cold water; drain. Combine crab meat, carrot, cucumber, onion, green pepper and sweet pickles in bowl; mix well. Combine French dressing, sour cream and mayonnaise in bowl; mix well. Add French dressing mixture, macaroni, salt and pepper to crab meat; mix well. Chill, covered, until serving time. Spoon into serving dish. **Yield: 12 servings.**

Approx Per Serving: Cal 421; Prot 12 g; Carbo 20 g; Fiber 2 g;
  T Fat 33 g; 69% Calories from Fat; Chol 63 mg; Sod 470 mg.

Wenham Tea House

Dilled Carrots

6 tablespoons sugar
1/2 teaspoon (or more) salt
5 cloves of garlic, minced
1/4 cup dillweed

6 small onions, chopped
6 cups each water and vinegar
3 1-pound packages carrots,
   julienned

Bring first 7 ingredients to a boil in saucepan, stirring frequently. Remove from heat. Arrange carrots in shallow dish. Add marinade. Marinate, covered, in refrigerator overnight; drain. **Yield: 12 servings.**

Approx Per Serving: Cal 110; Prot 2 g; Carbo 30 g; Fiber 5 g;
   T Fat <1 g; 3% Calories from Fat; Chol 0 mg; Sod 131 mg.

Wenham Tea House

Caesar Salad

2/3 cup olive oil
2 cloves of garlic, minced
1/2 cup vegetable oil
1 cup grated Italian cheese
11/2 teaspoons salt
6 tablespoons fresh lemon juice

1/8 teaspoon pepper
2 eggs
11/2 bunches Romaine lettuce
1 pound bacon, crisp-fried,
   crumbled
2 cups croutons

Blend olive oil, garlic and vegetable oil in blender. Add cheese, salt, lemon juice, pepper and eggs; process until mixed. Combine remaining ingredients in salad bowl. Add dressing; toss to mix. **Yield: 12 servings.**

Approx Per Serving: Cal 320; Prot 8 g; Carbo 6 g; Fiber 1 g;
   T Fat 30 g; 83% Calories from Fat; Chol 50 mg; Sod 653 mg.

Judy Hoyle, WVIS Member

Crisp Fresh Cucumber Pickles

11/2 cups cold water
11/2 cups vinegar
11/2 cups sugar
2 tablespoons onion flakes
1 teaspoon salt

1 teaspoon celery seed
3/4 teaspoon garlic salt
3/4 teaspoon onion salt
3/4 teaspoon celery salt
4 to 5 large cucumbers

Mix first 9 ingredients in 1/2-gallon jar. Shake, covered, until sugar is dissolved. Wash cucumbers; cut into 1/4-inch slices. Pack into jar; add marinade. Chill, covered, for several days. **Yield: 30 servings.**

Approx Per Serving: Cal 48; Prot <1 g; Carbo 12 g; Fiber 1 g;
   T Fat <1 g; 1% Calories from Fat; Chol 0 mg; Sod 226 mg.

Wenham Tea House

Arizona Salad

1 pound ground chuck
2 16-ounce cans kidney beans
1 head iceberg lettuce, shredded
4 tomatoes, chopped
3/4 cup finely chopped onion
8 ounces longhorn cheese,
    shredded

1 16-ounce package tortilla
    chips, crumbled
2 cups catsup
1 cup lemon juice
1/2 cup sugar
Garlic salt to taste

Brown ground beef in skillet, stirring until crumbly; drain. Add kidney beans; mix well. Remove from heat. Layer lettuce, tomatoes, ground chuck mixture, onion, cheese and tortilla chips in large glass bowl. Combine catsup, lemon juice, sugar and garlic salt in bowl; mix well. Serve with salad accompanied by French bread. **Yield: 8 servings.**

Approx Per Serving: Cal 748; Prot 30 g; Carbo 88 g; Fiber 13 g;
    T Fat 33 g; 39% Calories from Fat; Chol 67 mg; Sod 1601 mg.

Jean Eddy, Hobbs House Staff

Debbie's Salad

1 clove of garlic, peeled
6 slices crisp-fried bacon,
    crumbled
1 small onion, finely chopped
1/2 cup finely chopped sharp
    Cheddar cheese

3 hard-boiled eggs, finely
    chopped
1/2 cup celery, finely chopped
2 cups drained cooked peas
1 teaspoon MSG
1/2 cup mayonnaise

Rub bowl lightly with garlic. Combine next 7 ingredients in bowl; toss to mix. Let stand, covered, at room temperature for 1 hour. Add mayonnaise; mix well. Chill, covered, in refrigerator for 1 hour. Serve on lettuce-lined salad plates garnished with tomatoes. **Yield: 6 servings.**

Approx Per Serving: Cal 299; Prot 11 g; Carbo 11 g; Fiber 3 g;
    T Fat 24 g; 71% Calories from Fat; Chol 133 mg; Sod 1021 mg.

Joanne L. Potter, Hobbs House Staff

*For **Coleslaw Dressing**, bring 1/2 cup vinegar
and 1/2 cup sugar to a boil. Add a mixture of 1 beaten
egg and 1 cup sour cream and chill well.*

Layered Salad

1 head iceberg lettuce, shredded
2 cups sliced celery
2 green bell peppers, chopped
1 sweet onion, chopped
1 10-ounce package frozen peas, thawed

1 cup sour cream
1 cup mayonnaise
2 tablespoons sugar
4 ounces Cheddar cheese, shredded

Layer half the lettuce, celery, green peppers, onion, peas and remaining lettuce in large glass salad bowl. Combine sour cream, mayonnaise and sugar in bowl; mix well. Spread over layers; sprinkle with cheese. Chill, covered with plastic wrap, in refrigerator for 8 to 24 hours.
Yield: 10 servings.

Approx Per Serving: Cal 300; Prot 6 g; Carbo 11 g; Fiber 3 g;
T Fat 26 g; 77% Calories from Fat; Chol 35 mg; Sod 264 mg.

Dawn Schuster, WVIS Treasurer, Director

Spinach Salad

¼ cup oil
1 clove of garlic, sliced
¼ cup red wine vinegar
¼ cup lemon juice
½ teaspoon salt
Pepper to taste
2 tablespoons grated Italian cheese

1 1-pound package fresh spinach
1 hard-boiled egg, finely chopped
6 slices crisp-fried bacon, crumbled

Combine oil and garlic in bowl. Let stand at room temperature for 1 hour. Remove garlic; discard. Combine vinegar, lemon juice, salt and pepper in mixer bowl; beat well. Add oil in slow steady stream, beating constantly. Add cheese; beat well. Wash spinach; pat dry with paper towel. Cut spinach into bite-sized pieces. Combine spinach, egg and bacon in large salad bowl; mix well. Add dressing; toss to mix.
Yield: 8 servings.

Approx Per Serving: Cal 119; Prot 4 g; Carbo 3 g; Fiber 2 g;
T Fat 10 g; 75% Calories from Fat; Chol 32 mg; Sod 285 mg.

Wenham Tea House

Vegetable Mousse

2 cups canned stewed tomatoes
1 6-ounce package lemon
  gelatin
1 cup chopped celery
1/2 cup chopped green bell
  pepper

1 cup chopped cucumber
1/2 cup chopped scallions and
  tops
1 cup mayonnaise
2 tablespoons horseradish

Bring tomatoes to a boil in saucepan, stirring frequently. Remove from heat. Stir in gelatin until dissolved. Add celery, green pepper, cucumber and scallions; mix well. Mix mayonnaise and horseradish together in bowl. Add to vegetable mixture; mix well. Pour into mold. Chill until set. Unmold onto serving plate. Garnish with hard-boiled eggs and tomatoes. **Yield: 8 servings.**

Approx Per Serving: Cal 305; Prot 3 g; Carbo 27 g; Fiber 1 g;
  T Fat 22 g; 62% Calories from Fat; Chol 16 mg; Sod 422 mg.

Wenham Tea House

Wilted Dandelion Greens

4 to 5 ounces salt pork, chopped
Vinegar
5 to 6 tablespoons chopped
  onion
Salt and pepper to taste

2 tablespoons (about) flour
1 pound fresh dandelion greens
1 or 2 cold boiled potatoes,
  chopped

Sauté salt pork in skillet until crisp. Remove pork to paper towels to drain. Measure pan drippings. Add equal amount of vinegar to pan drippings. Combine vinegar mixture, onion, salt and pepper in skillet. Cook for 1 minute, stirring frequently. Stir in flour. Cook until slightly thickened. Wash greens; pat dry with paper towel. Place in bowl. Add hot dressing; toss to mix. Add potatoes and pork; toss to mix. May substitute spinach for dandelion greens. **Yield: 4 servings.**

Nutritional information for this recipe is not available.

Mary K. Polsonetti, WVIS Member and Volunteer

Bleu Cheese Dressing

1 cup mayonnaise
1 cup sour cream
1 tablespoon lemon juice
1 clove of garlic, minced

4 ounces bleu cheese, crumbled
2 teaspoons salt
4 teaspoons sugar

Combine mayonnaise, sour cream, lemon juice, garlic, bleu cheese, salt and sugar in bowl; mix well. May double recipe to make ½ gallon dressing but use the same amount of salt and sugar. Use 4 times each ingredient, including salt and sugar, to make 1 gallon dressing. **Yield: 32 (2-tablespoon) servings.**

Approx Per Serving: Cal 151; Prot 2 g; Carbo 2 g; Fiber <1 g;
    T Fat 16 g; 91% Calories from Fat; Chol 34 mg; Sod 449 mg.

Wenham Tea House

Celery Seed Dressing

½ cup sugar
1 teaspoon celery seed
1 teaspoon salt
1 teaspoon dry mustard

1 teaspoon paprika
⅓ cup lemon juice
¾ cup vegetable oil

Combine sugar, celery seed, salt, mustard, paprika and lemon juice in mixer bowl; mix well. Add oil in a slow steady stream, beating constantly. Serve with fruit salad. **Yield: 12 (2-tablespoon) servings.**

Approx Per Serving: Cal 157; Prot <1 g; Carbo 9 g; Fiber <1 g;
    T Fat 14 g; 80% Calories from Fat; Chol 0 mg; Sod 179 mg.

Wenham Tea House

Poppy Seed Dressing

1 egg
¼ cup sugar
1 tablespoon Dijon mustard
⅔ cup red wine vinegar

½ teaspoon salt
3 tablespoons grated onion
2 cups corn oil
3 tablespoons poppy seed

Combine egg, sugar, mustard, vinegar, salt and onion in blender container. Process at high speed for 1 minute. Add oil in a fine steady stream, processing constantly at high speed until well blended. Add poppy seed, processing until mixed. **Yield: 32 (2-tablespoon) servings.**

Approx Per Serving: Cal 135; Prot <1 g; Carbo 2 g; Fiber <1 g;
    T Fat 14 g; 93% Calories from Fat; Chol 7 mg; Sod 42 mg.

Wenham Tea House

Wenham Lake

Main Dishes

Beef Burgundy Pies

2 pounds round steak, cut into
  1-inch cubes
1/3 cup flour
2 teaspoons salt
1/2 teaspoon pepper
2 cloves of garlic, minced
1/3 cup oil
2 10-ounce cans beef broth
2 cups Burgundy wine
1/2 teaspoon each dried dillweed
  and marjoram, crushed
2 9-ounce packages frozen
  artichoke hearts
3 cups sliced mushrooms
1/3 cup flour
1/2 cup water
2 cups baking mix
2/3 cup milk

Coat round steak with mixture of 1/3 cup flour, salt and pepper. Brown with garlic in hot oil in saucepan. Add broth, wine and herbs. Simmer, covered, for 1 1/2 hours, stirring occasionally. Cook artichoke hearts using package directions; drain. Add artichoke hearts and mushrooms to beef mixture. Cook for 10 minutes. Blend 1/3 cup flour with water. Stir into beef mixture. Cook until thickened, stirring constantly. Pour into two 2-quart casseroles. Drop mixture of baking mix and milk by spoonfuls over top. Bake at 400 degrees for 12 minutes or until biscuits are brown. **Yield: 12 servings.**

Approx Per Serving: Cal 332; Prot 19 g; Carbo 26 g; Fiber 4 g;
  T Fat 14 g; 39% Calories from Fat; Chol 44 mg; Sod 828 mg.

Lee Nelson, Wenham Exchange Manager

Chinese Beef and Pea Pods

1 pound 1/4-inch thick round
  steak
1/2 teaspoon meat tenderizer
2 tablespoons oil
1 16-ounce can chop suey
  vegetables, drained
1 6-ounce can button
  mushrooms
1/4 cup soy sauce
1/4 cup water
2 tablespoons brown sugar
1/4 teaspoon ginger
1 7-ounce package frozen
  Chinese pea pods, thawed
1 1/2 teaspoons cornstarch
1/4 cup water

Sprinkle steak with meat tenderizer. Cut into 1/4-inch strips. Brown in hot oil in skillet for 30 seconds on each side; drain. Combine chop suey vegetables and undrained mushrooms in skillet. Add mixture of next 4 ingredients. Bring to a boil. Add pea pods. Cook, covered, for 1 minute. Blend cornstarch with 1/4 cup water. Stir into skillet. Cook until thickened, stirring constantly. Add steak. Heat to serving temperature. Serve over hot cooked rice. **Yield: 4 servings.**

Approx Per Serving: Cal 313; Prot 27 g; Carbo 20 g; Fiber 2 g;
  T Fat 14 g; 39% Calories from Fat; Chol 64 mg; Sod 2224 mg.

Wenham Tea House

Stifado

3 pounds lean stew beef
Salt and freshly ground pepper
    to taste
1/2 cup butter
3 to 4 large onions, sliced
1   6-ounce can tomato paste
1/3 cup cream sherry
2 tablespoons red wine vinegar

1 tablespoon brown sugar
1 clove of garlic, minced
1 bay leaf
1 stick cinnamon
1/2 teaspoon whole cloves
1/4 teaspoon ground cumin
2 tablespoons raisins

Cut beef into small cubes; season with salt and pepper. Cook in butter in skillet over low heat; do not brown. Spoon into slow cooker. Arrange onions over beef. Combine tomato paste, sherry, vinegar, brown sugar and garlic in small bowl. Pour over onions and beef. Add bay leaf, cinnamon, cloves, cumin and raisins. Simmer on Low for 3 hours. Remove bay leaf. Serve with tossed salad, red wine and Italian bread. **Yield: 6 servings.**

Approx Per Serving: Cal 568; Prot 45 g; Carbo 25 g; Fiber 3 g;
    T Fat 29 g; 48% Calories from Fat; Chol 169 mg; Sod 221 mg.

Mary S. Prahl, Hobbs House Staff

Perfect Beef Stroganoff

2 pounds filet of beef
6 tablespoons butter
1 cup chopped onion
1 clove of garlic, finely chopped
8 ounces fresh mushrooms,
    sliced 1/4-inch thick
3 tablespoons flour
2 teaspoons meat extract paste
1 tablespoon catsup
1/2 teaspoon salt

1/8 teaspoon pepper
1   10-ounce can beef bouillon
1/4 cup dry white wine
1 tablespoon snipped fresh dill
1 1/2 cups sour cream
1 1/2 cups cooked wild rice
4 cups cooked white rice
2 tablespoons chopped fresh
    dill or parsley

Trim fat from beef; cut crosswise into 1/2-inch slices. Cut each slice into 1/2-inch wide strips. Sear beef on all sides in 2 tablespoons butter in skillet over high heat; remove with tongs to platter. Sauté onion, garlic and mushrooms in remaining butter until onion is golden. Remove from heat. Add flour, meat extract, catsup, salt and pepper, stirring until smooth. Stir in bouillon gradually. Bring to a boil; reduce heat. Simmer for 5 minutes, stirring frequently. Add wine, dill and sour cream; mix well. Add beef. Simmer until heated through. Serve over mixture of wild and white rice. Sprinkle with 2 tablespoons dill. **Yield: 10 servings.**

Approx Per Serving: Cal 398; Prot 22 g; Carbo 32 g; Fiber 2 g;
    T Fat 20 g; 45% Calories from Fat; Chol 85 mg; Sod 323 mg.

Wenham Tea House

Beef and Eggplant Parmigiana

1/3 cup chopped onion
1 clove of garlic, crushed
1 1/2 pounds ground chuck
2 tablespoons margarine
3 8-ounce cans tomato sauce
3/4 tablespoon oregano
1 teaspoon basil
1/8 teaspoon anise seed
2 eggs, slightly beaten

1 tablespoon water
1/2 cup dry bread crumbs
1 cup grated Parmesan cheese
1 eggplant, cut into 1/4-inch
  slices
1/2 cup flour
2/3 cup oil
8 ounces mozzarella cheese,
  shredded

Cook onion, garlic and ground chuck in margarine in large skillet for 5 minutes, stirring frequently. Add tomato sauce, oregano, basil and anise seed; mix well. Simmer for 5 minutes, stirring frequently; set aside. Beat eggs with water in bowl. Combine bread crumbs and 1/2 cup Parmesan cheese in small bowl. Dip eggplant slices consecutively into flour, egg mixture and cheese mixture. Sauté in hot oil in skillet until brown on both sides, adding oil as needed. Alternate layers of eggplant, remaining Parmesan cheese, mozzarella cheese and meat sauce in greased 8x12-inch casserole until all ingredients are used, ending with mozzarella cheese. Bake at 350 degrees for 30 minutes or until cheese is melted and bubbly. **Yield: 6 servings.**

Approx Per Serving: Cal 687; Prot 37 g; Carbo 28 g; Fiber 4 g;
    T Fat 48 g; 62% Calories from Fat; Chol 164 mg; Sod 1238 mg.

Wenham Tea House

Cheeseburger Casserole

1/2 pound ground beef
1/4 cup chopped onion
1/4 cup chopped celery
1 green bell pepper, chopped
1 tablespoon prepared mustard
1/2 teaspoon salt
Worcestershire sauce to taste

8 slices bread, toasted
1 cup shredded Cheddar cheese
1 egg, beaten
3/4 cup milk
1/8 teaspoon dry mustard
1/2 teaspoon salt
Pepper to taste

Brown ground beef with onion, celery and green pepper in skillet, stirring frequently; drain well. Stir in prepared mustard, 1/2 teaspoon salt and Worcestershire sauce. Cut toast into triangles. Alternate layers of toast, cheese and ground beef mixture in baking dish, ending with cheese. Beat egg with remaining ingredients in bowl. Pour over layers. Garnish with paprika. Bake at 350 degrees for 45 minutes or until light brown. **Yield: 4 servings.**

Approx Per Serving: Cal 439; Prot 26 g; Carbo 32 g; Fiber 2 g;
    T Fat 23 g; 47% Calories from Fat; Chol 126 mg; Sod 1121 mg.

Wenham Tea House

Ham Loaf

1½ pounds ham and veal
2 eggs, beaten
¾ cup soft bread crumbs
¾ cup milk

Pepper to taste
2 teaspoons prepared mustard
¼ cup packed brown sugar
⅓ cup pineapple juice

Grind ham and veal together. Combine with eggs, bread crumbs, milk and pepper in bowl; mix well. Shape into loaf in foil-lined loaf pan. Combine mustard and brown sugar in small bowl; mix well. Spread over ham loaf. Drizzle pineapple juice over top. Bake at 350 degrees for 1½ hours, basting occasionally. Remove ham loaf to serving platter. Let stand for several minutes before slicing. May substitute fresh turkey for veal if desired. **Yield: 8 servings.**

Approx Per Serving: Cal 196; Prot 22 g; Carbo 13 g; Fiber <1 g; T Fat 6 g; 27% Calories from Fat; Chol 114 mg; Sod 654 mg.

Wenham Tea House

Asparagus-Ham Casserole

1 pound asparagus, fresh or
   frozen
3 tablespoons butter
3 tablespoons flour
½ teaspoon salt
Pepper to taste
¼ teaspoon dry mustard

1 teaspoon grated onion
1½ cups milk
1 cup cubed Cheddar cheese
2 tablespoons lemon juice
8 slices boiled ham
2 cups cooked rice

Cook asparagus in saucepan until tender-crisp. Keep warm. Melt butter in saucepan. Blend in flour, salt, pepper and mustard. Add onion. Cook over low heat for 2 to 3 minutes. Add milk gradually, stirring constantly. Cook until thickened, stirring constantly. Add cheese, stirring until melted. Drain asparagus; sprinkle with lemon juice. Roll up in ham slices. Line baking dish with rice. Arrange ham rolls over rice. Pour sauce over top. Broil 6 inches from heat source until golden brown. **Yield: 6 servings.**

Approx Per Serving: Cal 330; Prot 20 g; Carbo 26 g; Fiber 1 g; T Fat 16 g; 44% Calories from Fat; Chol 64 mg; Sod 871 mg.

Wenham Tea House

*Chop leftover ham and add to macaroni and
cheese, scrambled eggs, quiche or dried beans or lentils.*

Cauliflower and Ham Bake

1 medium head cauliflower
2 cups cubed cooked ham
1 3-ounce can sliced
   mushrooms, drained
2 tablespoons melted butter
2 tablespoons flour
1 cup milk
1 cup shredded Cheddar cheese
1/2 cup sour cream
1 tablespoon fine dry bread
   crumbs

Break cauliflower into flowerets. Cook in a small amount of boiling salted water until tender; drain. Combine with ham and mushrooms in bowl. Blend melted butter and flour in small saucepan. Stir in milk. Cook until thickened and bubbly, stirring constantly. Add cheese and sour cream. Cook until cheese melts, stirring constantly. Add to ham mixture; mix gently. Pour into 1 1/2-quart casserole. Sprinkle bread crumbs over top. Bake at 350 degrees for 40 minutes or until heated through. **Yield: 6 servings.**

Approx Per Serving: Cal 282; Prot 20 g; Carbo 10 g; Fiber 2 g;
   T Fat 18 g; 58% Calories from Fat; Chol 70 mg; Sod 873 mg.

Wenham Tea House

Ham and Cheese Strata

12 slices white bread
2 cups shredded Cheddar
   cheese
6 thin slices boiled ham
4 eggs, well beaten
2 1/2 cups milk
3/4 teaspoon salt
1/8 teaspoon pepper
1/2 teaspoon prepared mustard
2 teaspoons minced onion
   flakes
1/2 teaspoon Worcestershire
   sauce

Arrange half the bread slices in greased shallow 2-quart baking dish, cutting slices to fit. Sprinkle with cheese; top with ham slices. Place remaining bread over ham. Pour mixture of eggs and remaining ingredients over layers. Chill for 1 hour. Bake at 350 degrees for 1 hour or until knife inserted in center comes out clean. **Yield: 6 servings.**

Approx Per Serving: Cal 463; Prot 29 g; Carbo 34 g; Fiber 1 g;
   T Fat 23 g; 46% Calories from Fat; Chol 211 mg; Sod 1263 mg.

Wenham Tea House

Ham Divan

1 10-ounce package frozen
  broccoli
4 slices white bread
2 teaspoons butter
4 large thin slices baked ham

1 cup sour cream
1 teaspoon prepared mustard
1/2 cup shredded Cheddar
  cheese

Cook broccoli using package directions; drain. Toast bread and spread with butter. Layer in large shallow baking dish. Top with ham slices and broccoli. Combine sour cream and mustard in small bowl. Spoon in ribbons over broccoli. Sprinkle with cheese. Bake at 400 degrees for 15 minutes or until cheese is melted. **Yield: 4 servings.**

Approx Per Serving: Cal 337; Prot 17 g; Carbo 20 g; Fiber 3 g;
  T Fat 22 g; 56% Calories from Fat; Chol 61 mg; Sod 688 mg.

Wenham Tea House

Ham and Corn Quiche

1 8-count can crescent rolls
2 eggs, beaten
1 cup cubed ham
1 cup shredded Swiss cheese
1 to 1 1/2 cups drained whole
  kernel corn

1/2 cup evaporated milk
1/4 teaspoon onion salt
1/4 teaspoon thyme or basil
Parsley to taste

Separate crescent dough into 8 triangles; press into 9-inch pie plate. Seal edges to form crust. Combine eggs, ham, cheese, corn, evaporated milk, onion salt and thyme in bowl; mix well. Pour into prepared pie plate, spreading evenly. Sprinkle with parsley; cover edge of crust with foil. Bake at 350 degrees for 25 minutes. Remove foil. Bake for 15 to 20 minutes longer or until set. Cool for 5 minutes before serving.
Yield: 8 servings.

Approx Per Serving: Cal 247; Prot 13 g; Carbo 19 g; Fiber <1 g;
  T Fat 13 g; 48% Calories from Fat; Chol 81 mg; Sod 668 mg.

Wenham Tea House

Swiss Turkey-Ham Bake

1/2 cup chopped onion
2 tablespoons butter
3 tablespoons flour
1/2 teaspoon salt
1/4 teaspoon pepper
1 3-ounce can sliced
  mushrooms
1 cup light cream

2 tablespoons dry sherry
2 cups cubed cooked turkey
1 cup cubed cooked ham
1 5-ounce can sliced water
  chestnuts, drained
1/2 cup shredded Swiss cheese
11/2 cups soft bread crumbs
3 tablespoons melted butter

Sauté onion in 2 tablespoons butter in saucepan until tender. Add flour, salt and pepper, stirring until blended. Add undrained mushrooms, cream and sherry. Cook over medium heat until thick and bubbly, stirring constantly. Add turkey, ham and water chestnuts; mix well. Spoon into 11/2-quart casserole. Combine cheese, bread crumbs and melted butter in small bowl; mix well. Sprinkle around edges of casserole. Bake at 400 degrees for 25 minutes or until light brown. **Yield: 6 servings.**

Approx Per Serving: Cal 372; Prot 25 g; Carbo 15 g; Fiber 1 g;
  T Fat 23 g; 56% Calories from Fat; Chol 112 mg; Sod 712 mg.

Wenham Tea House

Eggplant Moussaka

1 medium eggplant, peeled, cut
  into 1/2-inch slices
5 tablespoons butter
1/2 cup chopped onion
3/4 pound lean ground lamb
3/4 teaspoon salt
Pepper to taste

1 8-ounce can tomato sauce
3 tablespoons melted butter
1/2 cup fine dry bread crumbs
1/3 cup grated Parmesan cheese
8 ounces mozzarella cheese, cut
  into 1/4-inch slices

Cook eggplant in skillet in 2 tablespoons butter until light brown on both sides, adding additional butter as needed. Drain on paper towels. Sauté onion and lamb in skillet over medium high heat until lamb is brown and onion is tender, stirring occasionally. Season with salt and pepper. Layer 1/3 of the eggplant, half the lamb mixture and half the tomato sauce in shallow 2-quart casserole until all ingredients are used, ending with eggplant. Combine melted butter, bread crumbs and Parmesan cheese in small bowl; mix well. Sprinkle over eggplant layer. Bake at 350 degrees for 20 minutes. Place mozzarella cheese over top. Bake for 10 minutes longer. **Yield: 6 servings.**

Approx Per Serving: Cal 433; Prot 25 g; Carbo 18 g; Fiber 5 g;
  T Fat 29 g; 60% Calories from Fat; Chol 114 mg; Sod 950 mg.

Wenham Tea House

Spring Lamb Stew with Dill

2½ pounds boneless lamb, fat trimmed, cut into 1-inch cubes
2 tablespoons oil
12 small white onions
10 cups water
1 6-ounce can tomato juice
2 teaspoons salt
¼ teaspoon pepper
6 medium carrots
6 new potatoes
¼ cup flour
1 10-ounce package frozen peas
Fresh dill to taste

Sauté lamb in hot oil in large saucepan ⅓ at a time until brown. Remove to warm platter. Add onions. Cook until brown; remove and set aside. Drain saucepan. Return lamb to saucepan. Add 10 cups water, tomato juice, salt and pepper. Bring to a boil; reduce heat. Simmer, covered, for 30 minutes. Scrape carrots; cut into halves. Cut ½-inch wide strip of peel from center of each potato. Add onions, carrots and potatoes to pan with lamb. Simmer, covered, for 40 minutes or until vegetables are tender. Remove from heat; skim. Combine flour with enough water to make stew of desired consistency. Stir into pan juices. Add peas and dill. Simmer, covered, for 10 to 15 minutes or until peas are tender. Remove from heat; let stand for 5 minutes. Skim surface. Ladle into heated serving dish. **Yield: 6 servings.**

Approx Per Serving: Cal 533; Prot 42 g; Carbo 54 g; Fiber 10 g;
    T Fat 16 g; 28% Calories from Fat; Chol 106 mg; Sod 997 mg.

Wenham Tea House

Pork Curry Hot Pot

2 pounds lean boneless pork, cut into 1-inch cubes
2 tablespoons shortening
1½ cups sliced onion
1 cup peeled, chopped apple
3 tablespoons flour
1 teaspoon salt
Curry powder to taste
¼ teaspoon pepper
¼ teaspoon nutmeg
1 10-ounce can beef broth
1 16-ounce can tomatoes
⅓ cup seedless raisins
2 tablespoons brown sugar

Brown pork in hot shortening in large saucepan. Add onion and apple. Cook until onion is tender. Add flour, salt, curry powder, pepper and nutmeg, stirring to blend. Add beef broth, tomatoes, raisins and brown sugar; mix well. Simmer, covered, for 1¼ hours or until pork is tender. Serve over hot fluffy rice with flaked coconut, chutney, chopped peanuts, chopped green onions, lemon wedges, chopped green pepper and candied ginger. **Yield: 6 servings.**

Approx Per Serving: Cal 352; Prot 32 g; Carbo 23 g; Fiber 2 g;
    T Fat 15 g; 37% Calories from Fat; Chol 93 mg; Sod 709 mg.

Wenham Tea House

Pasta Sauce

2 cloves of garlic, chopped
1 onion, chopped
1/4 cup olive oil
Salt and pepper to taste
1/3 cup chopped fresh basil
1/3 teaspoon garlic powder
1/3 teaspoon onion powder
1/3 teaspoon pepper
1/3 teaspoon Italian seasoning
1   28-ounce can tomato sauce
2   6-ounce cans tomato paste
6 cups water
6 ounces blush wine
2 tablespoons sugar

1 1/2 pounds sweet Italian
  sausage
1 1/2 pounds ground beef
2/3 cup bread crumbs
4 slices Italian bread
1/2 cup water
2 tablespoons catsup
1 egg, beaten
1 teaspoon garlic salt
1 teaspoon onion salt
1/2 teaspoon pepper
2 tablespoons minced parsley
1   16-ounce package ziti
1/2 cup grated Parmesan cheese

Sauté garlic and onion in oil in large saucepan until golden; season with salt and pepper to taste. Combine next 10 ingredients in large bowl; mix well. Pour into saucepan. Simmer for 30 minutes. Pierce sausage with fork several times. Place on rack in broiler pan. Broil 6 inches from heat source until brown. Add to sauce. Simmer for 30 minutes. Combine ground beef and next 9 ingredients in bowl; mix well. Shape into meatballs. Place on rack in broiler pan. Broil 6 inches from heat source until brown. Add to sauce. Simmer for 30 minutes. Cook ziti using package directions; drain. Place in large serving bowl. Pour 2 cups sauce over ziti. Sprinkle with Parmesan cheese; mix well. Serve remaining sauce with sausauge and meatballs in separate serving dish. **Yield: 8 servings.**

Approx Per Serving: Cal 778; Prot 37 g; Carbo 79 g; Fiber 7 g;
    T Fat 34 g; 39% Calories from Fat; Chol 115 mg; Sod 1906 mg.

Jean M. Pantano, Hobbs House Staff

Chicken Bleu

8 chicken breasts
Salt and pepper to taste
1/2 cup butter

4 cups sour cream
1 pound bleu cheese, crumbled
1 clove of garlic, minced

Rinse chicken; pat dry. Season chicken with salt and pepper. Brown on both sides in butter in skillet. Arrange in shallow baking dish. Pour mixture of sour cream, bleu cheese and garlic over chicken. Bake at 350 degrees for 40 to 45 minutes or until chicken is tender. **Yield: 8 servings.**

Approx Per Serving: Cal 689; Prot 42 g; Carbo 6 g; Fiber <1 g;
    T Fat 55 g; 72% Calories from Fat; Chol 196 mg; Sod 1012 mg.

Wenham Tea House

Chicken à la Chicken

3 whole chicken breasts, split
Paprika to taste
2 tomatoes, sliced
2 10-ounce cans cream of
  mushroom soup

1 soup can water
1 teaspoon poultry seasoning
Salt and pepper to taste

Rinse chicken; pat dry. Arrange chicken breasts skin side down in baking dish. Bake at 400 degrees for 20 minutes. Sprinkle with paprika. Add tomatoes. Mix soup, water, poultry seasoning, salt and pepper together in bowl. Pour over chicken. Bake at 400 degrees for 20 minutes longer or until chicken is tender. May substitute milk for water. **Yield: 6 servings.**

Approx Per Serving: Cal 246; Prot 28 g; Carbo 9 g; Fiber 1 g;
  T Fat 10 g; 38% Calories from Fat; Chol 73 mg; Sod 832 mg.

Wenham Tea House

Chicken Breasts Extravaganza

8 chicken breasts filets
1/4 cup flour
1 clove of garlic, minced
1 teaspoon paprika
1 teaspoon salt
1/2 teaspoon pepper
2 tablespoons oil
1 chicken bouillon cube
1/4 cup hot water

2 teaspoons cornstarch
1 cup half and half
1 cup vermouth
1 teaspoon grated lemon rind
1 tablespoon lemon juice
3/4 cup shredded Cheddar
  cheese
1/4 cup chopped parsley

Rinse chicken; pat dry. Place in plastic bag. Mix flour, garlic, paprika, salt and pepper together. Add to chicken. Seal bag; shake to coat chicken. Brown chicken on both sides in hot oil in skillet. Dissolve bouillon in hot water. Add to chicken. Simmer, covered, for 30 minutes. Arrange chicken in single layer in shallow baking dish. Mix cornstarch with 1/4 of the half and half in bowl. Add to pan drippings; mix well. Add remaining half and half, vermouth, lemon rind and lemon juice; mix well. Cook for 3 minutes, stirring constantly. Pour over chicken. Bake, covered, at 350 degrees for 30 minutes. Remove cover. Sprinkle chicken with cheese and parsley. Bake at 350 degrees for 5 minutes longer. **Yield: 8 servings.**

Approx Per Serving: Cal 309; Prot 31 g; Carbo 7 g; Fiber <1 g;
  T Fat 14 g; 39% Calories from Fat; Chol 95 mg; Sod 558 mg.

Zetta J. Herrick, Past President, Wenham Museum

Chicken en Croûte

6 chicken breasts filets
1½ cups chicken broth
½ cup sherry
6 thin slices cooked ham
Dijon mustard to taste

Tarragon to taste
6 thin slices Swiss cheese
6 frozen puff pastry shells,
  thawed

Poach chicken in broth and wine in shallow saucepan for 15 minutes or until tender. Cool in cooking liquid; drain. Wrap each chicken breast in 1 ham slice; coat with mustard. Sprinkle with tarragon; wrap in cheese slice. Roll each puff pastry shell to 4-inch circle on lightly floured surface. Place 1 chicken breast on each pastry; moisten edges of pastry. Fold to enclose chicken, sealing edges. Place on ungreased baking sheet. Bake at 400 degrees for 20 minutes or until puffed and golden brown. Serve warm or cold. **Yield: 6 servings.**

Approx Per Serving: Cal 588; Prot 47 g; Carbo 24 g; Fiber 0 g;
  T Fat 30 g; 49% Calories from Fat; Chol 114 mg; Sod 1003 mg.

Susan LeTourneau, Vice President WVIS

Danish Chicken and Meatballs au Gratin

¾ pound ground veal
¼ cup flour
1 egg
⅛ teaspoon salt
Pepper to taste
2 teaspoons grated onion
½ cup milk
1 cup butter
6 chicken breasts filets

2 tablespoons butter
2 tablespoons flour
¼ teaspoon Dijon mustard
½ cup whipping cream
⅔ cup chicken broth
⅓ cup dry white wine
1 cup shredded Danish Samsoe
1 4-ounce jar sliced pimentos,
  drained

Combine first 7 ingredients in bowl; mix well. Let stand, covered, for 5 minutes. Drop by rounded teaspoonfuls several at a time into 1 cup hot butter in skillet. Cook for 4 minutes or just until brown; drain on paper towels. Rinse chicken; pat dry. Cut into ¼-inch strips. Cook in pan drippings until tender; remove to bowl. Heat 2 tablespoons butter, 2 tablespoons flour and mustard in saucepan. Cook until bubbly, stirring constantly. Stir in cream, broth and wine gradually. Cook until slightly thickened, stirring constantly. Add cheese gradually, stirring until melted. Add pimentos, chicken and meatballs. Cook until heated through. Spoon into ovenproof serving dish. Broil 5 inches from heat source for 2 minutes or until top is bubbly but not brown. Garnish with sautéed mushroom caps, cherry tomatoes and parsley. **Yield: 6 servings.**

Approx Per Serving: Cal 741; Prot 50 g; Carbo 9 g; Fiber 1 g;
  T Fat 55 g; 68% Calories from Fat; Chol 310 mg; Sod 614 mg.

Barbara Elliott, President, WVIS

Danish Chicken

1 clove of garlic, minced
1/3 teaspoon (or more) salt
Cayenne pepper to taste
6 chicken breasts
3 tablespoons butter
1 2¼-ounce package slivered
   almonds

2 cups seedless grapes
1½ cups half and half
1 tablespoon cornstarch
8 ounces sliced Havarti cheese

Mash garlic, salt and cayenne pepper into paste in bowl. Spread on chicken. Brown chicken on both sides in butter in skillet. Remove to baking dish. Sauté almonds in pan drippings. Sprinkle over chicken. Bake at 350 degrees for 40 to 45 minutes or until chicken is tender. Drain drippings into skillet. Turn off oven. Arrange grapes on baked chicken. Keep warm in oven. Add mixture of half and half and cornstarch to drippings in skillet, stirring to mix. Cook until thickened, stirring constantly. Break cheese into pieces; add to skillet gradually. Cook for 10 minutes or until cheese is melted. Arrange chicken on serving dish. Pour half of the sauce over chicken and serve remaining sauce in gravy boat. **Yield: 6 servings.**

Approx Per Serving: Cal 540; Prot 39 g; Carbo 16 g; Fiber 2 g;
    T Fat 36 g; 59% Calories from Fat; Chol 156 mg; Sod 450 mg.

Wenham Tea House

Chicken Dijonnaise

2 chicken breasts filets
1/2 cup Dijon-style mustard
1/3 cup white wine

1/3 cup nonfat plain yogurt
Tarragon to taste
Freshly ground pepper to taste

Rinse chicken; pat dry. Spread mustard on both sides of chicken; place in Dutch oven. Marinate, covered, in refrigerator for 2 hours or longer. Bake, uncovered, at 350 degrees for 30 to 40 minutes or until tender. Remove chicken to serving dish; keep warm. Scrape off mustard; place in Dutch oven. Add white wine and yogurt; mix well. Cook over low heat until thickened, stirring constantly. Add tarragon and pepper; mix well. Serve over chicken. May add additional mustard and wine to sauce. **Yield: 2 servings.**

Approx Per Serving: Cal 234; Prot 32 g; Carbo 7 g; Fiber <1 g;
    T Fat 6 g; 22% Calories from Fat; Chol 73 mg; Sod 876 mg.

Gynna Ames, WVIS Friend

Chicken Divan

2 10-ounce packages frozen
   broccoli
4 whole chicken breasts, cooked
1/4 cup butter
5 tablespoons flour
1 cup milk
1 cup whipping cream

1 cup shredded Cheddar cheese
Salt and pepper to taste
2 tablespoons sherry
1/2 cup bread crumbs
1/4 cup melted butter
1/2 cup grated Parmesan cheese

Cook broccoli using package directions. Layer chicken and broccoli in casserole. Melt 1/4 cup butter in skillet. Add flour, stirring until mixed. Add milk and cream. Cook until thickened, stirring constantly. Stir in Cheddar cheese until melted. Add salt, pepper and sherry; mix well. Pour over layers. Mix bread crumbs and melted butter in bowl. Sprinkle over cheese sauce. Top with Parmesan cheese. Bake at 350 degrees for 45 minutes. **Yield: 8 servings.**

Approx Per Serving: Cal 510; Prot 37 g; Carbo 15 g; Fiber 2 g;
   T Fat 33 g; 59% Calories from Fat; Chol 167 mg; Sod 429 mg.

Wenham Tea House

French Chicken in Orange-Sherry Sauce

3 whole chicken breasts, split
1/2 teaspoon salt
1 medium onion, sliced
1/4 cup chopped green bell
   pepper
1 cup sliced mushrooms
1 teaspoon grated orange rind
1 cup orange juice
1/2 cup dry sherry

1/4 cup water
1 tablespoon brown sugar
1 teaspoon salt
1/4 teaspoon pepper
1 tablespoon flour
2 teaspoons chopped parsley
Paprika to taste
Sections of 1 orange

Rinse chicken; pat dry. Place skin side up on rack in broiler pan. Broil 2-inches from heat source for 10 minutes or until skin is brown and crackly. Do not turn. Place chicken in shallow 2-quart baking dish. Sprinkle with 1/2 teaspoon salt, onion, green pepper and mushrooms. Combine orange rind, orange juice, sherry, water, brown sugar, 1 teaspoon salt, pepper and flour in saucepan; mix well. Cook over medium heat until thickened, stirring constantly. Stir in parsley. Pour over chicken. Bake at 375 degrees for 45 minutes or until chicken is tender, basting several times. Sprinkle with paprika. Garnish with orange sections. **Yield: 6 servings.**

Approx Per Serving: Cal 223; Prot 28 g; Carbo 14 g; Fiber 2 g;
   T Fat 3 g; 13% Calories from Fat; Chol 72 mg; Sod 601 mg.

Wenham Tea House

Chicken Marsala

2 small whole chicken breasts,
  boned, skinned
1/2 cup flour
2 tablespoons butter
5 ounces Marsala
2 tablespoons chicken broth

5 ounces fresh mushrooms,
  sliced
2 tablespoons butter
2 tablespoons finely chopped
  parsley

Rinse chicken; pat dry. Cut chicken into 12 pieces. Roll in flour to coat. Brown chicken on both sides in 2 tablespoons butter in skillet. Add wine. Cook until reduced by 1/3. Add chicken broth, mushrooms and remaining 2 tablespoons butter. Cook until butter is melted. Remove chicken to serving plate. Keep warm. Cook sauce until thickened, stirring constantly. Pour over chicken. Garnish with parsley. **Yield: 4 servings.**

Approx Per Serving: Cal 276; Prot 13 g; Carbo 18 g; Fiber 1 g;
  T Fat 13 g; 42% Calories from Fat; Chol 58 mg; Sod 150 mg.

Ruth C. Smith, Chairman, Volunteers

Breasts of Chicken Paprika

6 whole chicken breasts, split,
  skinned
2 tablespoons butter
16 small white onions
1 cup chopped onion
2 tablespoons butter
8 small carrots

2 10-ounce cans chicken broth
2 tablespoons paprika
2 teaspoons salt
1/3 cup flour
1/2 cup dry white wine
2 cups sour cream

Rinse chicken; pat dry. Brown chicken 1/2 at a time in 2 tablespoons butter in large heavy skillet. Remove to dish. Sauté whole onions and chopped onion in remaining 2 tablespoons butter and pan drippings until light brown. Cut carrots into 1 1/2-inch pieces. Add to onions in skillet. Sauté for 1 to 2 minutes. Add chicken broth, paprika and salt; mix well. Return chicken to skillet, overlapping pieces. Simmer, covered, for 15 minutes. Rearrange chicken. Simmer, covered, for 25 minutes or until chicken is tender. Remove chicken to serving platter. Keep warm. Blend flour and wine together in bowl. Add to broth mixture. Bring to a boil; reduce heat. Simmer for 2 minutes, stirring constantly. Remove from heat. Add sour cream gradually. Heat to serving temperature. Do not boil. Pour over chicken. Garnish with parsley. Chicken may be prepared ahead and frozen. Add sour cream after reheating. **Yield: 12 servings.**

Approx Per Serving: Cal 360; Prot 32 g; Carbo 22 g; Fiber 4 g;
  T Fat 16 g; 40% Calories from Fat; Chol 100 mg; Sod 638 mg.

Wenham Tea House

Pecan Chicken

2 cups buttermilk
2 eggs, beaten
2 cups flour
2 cups ground pecans
3/4 cup sesame seed
2 tablespoons salt

2 tablespoons paprika
Pepper to taste
8 chicken breasts, boned
1 cup margarine
3/4 cup pecan halves

Combine buttermilk and eggs in shallow bowl; mix well. Combine flour, ground pecans, sesame seed, salt, paprika and pepper in shallow bowl; mix well. Rinse chicken. Dip chicken in buttermilk mixture; roll in flour mixture to coat. Fry chicken in margarine in large skillet until golden brown and tender. Remove to serving plate. Garnish with pecan halves. Serve with mustard sauce. **Yield: 8 servings.**

Approx Per Serving: Cal 856; Prot 41 g; Carbo 37 g; Fiber 5 g;
    T Fat 63 g; 65% Calories from Fat; Chol 128 mg; Sod 2018 mg.

Wenham Tea House

Poppy Seed Chicken

2 to 3 pounds chicken breasts,
    boned
1 cup sour cream
1   10-ounce can cream of
    chicken soup

1½ cups crushed butter
    crackers
1 tablespoon poppy seed
½ cup melted butter

Rinse chicken; pat dry. Place in casserole. Mix sour cream and soup in bowl. Pour over chicken. Combine cracker crumbs, poppy seed and butter in bowl; mix well. Sprinkle over chicken. Bake at 350 degrees for 25 to 30 minutes or until chicken is tender. **Yield: 6 servings.**

Approx Per Serving: Cal 655; Prot 57 g; Carbo 20 g; Fiber <1 g;
    T Fat 40 g; 53% Calories from Fat; Chol 207 mg; Sod 858 mg.

Bette Hatch, Tea House Staff

*Make **Dressed-Up Chicken Dish** by coating chicken pieces
with flour, salt and pepper and browning in margarine.
Combine with 1 can of cream of mushroom soup, ½ soup
can water and ½ cup white wine in baking pan
and bake at 325 degrees for 1 hour.*

Raspberry Chicken

2 tablespoons flour
Salt to taste
4 chicken breasts, boned,
  skinned
1½ tablespoons butter

1 tablespoon oil
6 tablespoons raspberry vinegar
¾ cup chicken broth
½ cup whipping cream

Mix flour and salt in shallow bowl. Rinse chicken; pat dry. Roll chicken in mixture until coated. Brown chicken on both sides in butter and oil in skillet. Remove chicken to plate. Add vinegar and chicken broth to pan drippings; stir to mix. Add chicken. Simmer, uncovered, for 10 to 15 minutes, or until chicken is tender. Remove chicken to serving platter. Cook pan liquid over high heat until reduced, stirring constantly. Add cream. Cook until of desired thickness, stirring constantly. Pour over chicken. **Yield: 4 servings.**

Approx Per Serving: Cal 336; Prot 28 g; Carbo 5 g; Fiber <1 g;
  T Fat 22 g; 59% Calories from Fat; Chol 125 mg; Sod 256 mg.

Wenham Tea House

Chicken Sour Cream

2 cups sour cream
2 tablespoons lemon juice
2 teaspoons Worcestershire
  sauce
¼ teaspoon crushed celery seed
1 teaspoon paprika
1 clove of garlic, minced
½ teaspoon salt
⅛ teaspoon pepper

8 chicken breasts
1 8-ounce package
  herb-flavored stuffing mix
½ cup melted butter
1 10-ounce can golden
  mushroom soup
¼ cup chopped parsley
1 to 2 tablespoons sherry

Combine sour cream, lemon juice, Worcestershire sauce, celery seed, paprika, garlic, salt and pepper in bowl; mix well. Rinse chicken; pat dry and place in marinade. Marinate, covered, in refrigerator overnight. Drain chicken. Roll in stuffing mix to coat; place in greased casserole. Drizzle butter over chicken. Bake at 350 degrees for 1 hour. Combine soup, parsley and sherry in bowl; pour over chicken. Bake for 5 minutes longer or until soup mixture is heated to serving temperature. **Yield: 8 servings.**

Approx Per Serving: Cal 514; Prot 33 g; Carbo 27 g; Fiber <1 g;
  T Fat 30 g; 54% Calories from Fat; Chol 129 mg; Sod 1002 mg.

Wenham Tea House

Oriental Chicken with Vegetables

8 ounces boneless chicken breasts
1 chicken bouillon cube
1 cup boiling water
2 tablespoons vegetable oil
1 green bell pepper, seeded, thinly sliced
4 ounces fresh mushrooms, sliced
1 medium onion, thinly sliced

2 cups diagonally sliced celery
1 5-ounce can sliced water chestnuts, drained
1/2 teaspoon salt
1/4 teaspoon ground ginger
1 teaspoon MSG
2 teaspoons cornstarch
2 tablespoons soy sauce
2 cups hot cooked rice

Rinse chicken; pat dry. Cut into thin strips. Dissolve bouillon cube in boiling water. Heat oil in medium skillet over medium-high heat. Add chicken strips. Stir-fry for 2 to 3 minutes or until lightly browned. Add vegetables, seasonings and bouillon. Cook, covered, over medium-low heat for 10 minutes. Dissolve cornstarch in soy sauce. Stir into skillet. Cook for 5 minutes or until pan juices are thickened and clear, stirring constantly. Serve over hot cooked rice. **Yield: 3 servings.**

Approx Per Serving: Cal 408; Prot 24 g; Carbo 52 g; Fiber 5 g; T Fat 12 g; 26% Calories from Fat; Chol 49 mg; Sod 2974 mg.

Wenham Tea House

Sweet and Sour Chicken

1 8-ounce bottle of Russian salad dressing
1 10-ounce jar apricot preserves

1 envelope dry onion soup mix
1/4 cup vinegar
1/4 cup water
4 whole chicken breasts, split

Mix first 5 ingredients in bowl. Rinse chicken; pat dry. Place in buttered casserole. Pour sauce over chicken. Bake at 350 degrees for 1 1/2 hours, basting twice. Serve with hot cooked rice. **Yield: 6 servings.**

Approx Per Serving: Cal 506; Prot 36 g; Carbo 38 g; Fiber 1 g; T Fat 23 g; 41% Calories from Fat; Chol 121 mg; Sod 522 mg.

Wenham Tea House

Stir a little peanut butter into medium white sauce for a new version of creamed chicken.

Wok Chicken

3/4 pound chicken breasts,
    boned
1/2 teaspoon salt
2 tablespoons wine
1 large egg white
2 teaspoons cornstarch
1/2 cup vegetable oil

2 cloves of garlic, minced
1/2 teaspoon ginger
3 scallions, chopped
1 green bell pepper, cut into
    strips
1 red bell pepper, cut into strips

Rinse chicken; pat dry. Cut into 1/4-inch strips. Place in shallow dish. Combine salt, wine, egg white and cornstarch in bowl; mix well. Pour over chicken. Marinate, covered, in refrigerator for 30 minutes or longer. Heat oil in wok. Add chicken. Stir-fry for 3 to 5 minutes or until cooked through. Remove chicken with slotted spoon to plate. Keep chicken warm. Add garlic, ginger and scallions to pan drippings; mix well. Add green and red peppers. Stir-fry for 5 minutes. Add chicken. Stir-fry until heated to serving temperature. Serve over rice. **Yield: 4 servings.**

Approx Per Serving: Cal 374; Prot 21 g; Carbo 4 g; Fiber 1 g;
    T Fat 30 g; 72% Calories from Fat; Chol 54 mg; Sod 328 mg.

Judy Morris, WVIS Member

Walnut Chicken

1 tablespoon vegetable oil
2 teaspoons soy sauce
1 teaspoon cornstarch
2 whole chicken breasts,
    boned, skinned
1/2 cup chicken broth
1/2 teaspoon ground ginger
1 tablespoon soy sauce
2 teaspoons cornstarch
1/2 teaspoon dried red pepper

1/4 cup vegetable oil
1 medium onion, cut into
    1-inch pieces
1 clove of garlic, minced
1 red bell pepper, cut into
    1-inch pieces
1/2 pound broccoli, cut into
    1-inch pieces
1/2 cup chopped walnuts
2 cups hot cooked rice

Mix first 3 ingredients in bowl. Rinse chicken; pat dry. Cut into 1-inch pieces. Add to marinade, stirring to coat. Marinate, covered, in refrigerator for 30 minutes. Combine broth and next 3 ingredients in bowl; mix well. Stir-fry chicken and dried red pepper in hot 1/4 cup oil in skillet until chicken is tender. Remove chicken with slotted spoon to plate. Stir-fry onion, garlic and red bell pepper in pan drippings until onion is tender. Add broccoli. Stir-fry until tender. Add chicken and broth mixture. Simmer until thickened, stirring constantly. Stir in walnuts. Serve over hot cooked rice. **Yield: 4 servings.**

Approx Per Serving: Cal 549; Prot 34 g; Carbo 37 g; Fiber 4 g;
    T Fat 30 g; 49% Calories from Fat; Chol 72 mg; Sod 607 mg.

Wenham Tea House

Easy Chicken and Rice

1 cup uncooked rice
1 10-ounce can mushroom
  soup
1¹/₂ soup cans milk

1 envelope onion soup mix
2¹/₂ pounds chicken pieces
Salt and pepper to taste

Combine rice, soup, milk and onion soup mix in 3-quart casserole; mix well. Place chicken skin side down on top of mixture. Bake, uncovered, at 250 degrees for 3 hours, turning chicken once. **Yield: 4 servings.**

Approx Per Serving: Cal 580; Prot 49 g; Carbo 49 g; Fiber 1 g;
    T Fat 20 g; 31% Calories from Fat; Chol 142 mg; Sod 899 mg.

Rita Kelley, Tea House Staff

Lemon-Ginger Chicken

2¹/₂ pounds chicken pieces
1 cup fresh lemon juice
4 cloves of garlic, minced
4 teaspoons finely chopped
  gingerroot
1 teaspoon lemon extract
1 cup flour
2 teaspoons ground ginger

1 teaspoon paprika
1 teaspoon salt
1 teaspoon pepper
2 cups vegetable oil
¹/₄ cup chicken broth
¹/₄ cup packed light brown
  sugar
2 lemons, thinly sliced

Rinse chicken; pat dry. Place in shallow bowl. Combine lemon juice, garlic, gingerroot and lemon extract in bowl; mix well. Pour over chicken, tossing to coat chicken. Marinate, covered, in refrigerator for 2 hours. Drain chicken, reserving marinade. Pat chicken dry. Combine flour, ground ginger, paprika, salt and pepper in plastic bag; shake, tightly closed, to mix. Add chicken; shake, tightly closed, to coat chicken. Heat oil in deep fryer to 375 degrees. Add chicken, several pieces at a time. Deep-fry until golden brown. Remove chicken; place skin side up in shallow baking dish. Add chicken broth and reserved marinade. Sprinkle with brown sugar, pressing lightly. Arrange lemon slices on top. Bake at 350 degrees for 40 to 45 minutes or until chicken is tender, basting once. **Yield: 4 servings.**

Approx Per Serving: Cal 491; Prot 46 g; Carbo 52 g; Fiber 2 g;
    T Fat 11 g; 21% Calories from Fat; Chol 127 mg; Sod 714 mg.
    Nutritional information does not include oil for deep-frying.

Wenham Tea House

Orange Marmalade Chicken

1 cup flour
1/2 teaspoon salt
1/2 teaspoon pepper
6 pounds chicken pieces
1/4 cup oil

2 cups fresh orange juice
1/4 cup soy sauce
11/2 teaspoons ginger
1/2 cup orange marmalade

Mix flour, salt and pepper together in shallow bowl. Rinse chicken; pat dry. Dredge chicken in flour until coated. Brown chicken on both sides in hot oil in skillet. Combine orange juice, soy sauce and ginger in bowl; mix well. Pour over chicken. Simmer, covered, for 30 minutes. Remove chicken to plate. Add marmalade to pan drippings, stirring to mix. Return chicken to skillet. Simmer until sauce is thickened and chicken is tender, stirring frequently. May brown coated chicken on baking sheet in 350-degree oven for 10 minutes. **Yield: 10 servings.**

Approx Per Serving: Cal 421; Prot 41 g; Carbo 27 g; Fiber 1 g;
 T Fat 16 g; 34% Calories from Fat; Chol 121 mg; Sod 639 mg.

Wenham Tea House

Chicken Sauté Chasseur

1/2 cup flour
Salt, pepper and thyme to taste
21/2 to 3 pounds chicken pieces
1/4 cup butter
1/4 cup chopped shallots

4 ounces mushrooms, chopped
1/2 cup white wine
3/4 cup canned tomatoes
2 tablespoons chopped parsley
Tarragon to taste

Combine flour, salt, pepper and thyme in shallow bowl; mix well. Rinse chicken; pat dry. Dredge in flour until coated. Brown chicken on both sides in butter in skillet. Add shallots, mushrooms, wine, tomatoes, parsley and tarragon. Simmer, covered, for 30 to 40 minutes or until chicken is tender, stirring occasionally. May substitute onions for shallots. **Yield: 6 servings.**

Approx Per Serving: Cal 350; Prot 35 g; Carbo 11 g; Fiber 1 g;
 T Fat 16 g; 44% Calories from Fat; Chol 122 mg; Sod 213 mg.

Wenham Tea House

*Prepare **Super Easy Chicken Bake** by layering 1 cup uncooked rice, chicken pieces and 1 envelope dry onion soup mix in a baking dish and pouring 4 cups chicken broth over the top. Bake at 375 degrees for 1 hour.*

Chicken Fiesta

6 frozen patty shells
2 tablespoons butter
1½ tablespoons flour
1⅓ cups half and half
⅓ cup dry sherry
½ teaspoon salt
¼ teaspoon paprika
⅛ teaspoon pepper

2½ cups chopped cooked
  chicken
¾ cup sliced fresh mushrooms
¾ cup shredded carrot
⅓ cup chopped green bell
  pepper
Chopped parsley to taste

Bake patty shells using package directions. Melt butter in skillet. Stir in flour until mixed. Cook for 1 to 2 minutes, stirring constantly. Remove from heat. Add half and half and sherry, stirring until smooth. Cook over low heat for 5 to 7 minutes or until thickened, stirring constantly. Add salt, paprika, pepper, chicken, mushrooms, carrot and green pepper. Simmer for 10 to 15 minutes or until vegetables are tender. Spoon into warm patty shells; sprinkle with parsley. **Yield: 6 servings.**

Approx Per Serving: Cal 497; Prot 23 g; Carbo 21 g; Fiber 1 g;
  T Fat 34 g; 64% Calories from Fat; Chol 82 mg; Sod 511 mg.

Wenham Tea House

Georgian Chicken

10 frozen patty shells
8 ounces fresh mushrooms,
  sliced
2 cups chicken broth
2 cups half and half
½ cup flour
1 teaspoon salt
¼ teaspoon pepper

1 teaspoon chopped green
  onions
2½ teaspoons chopped parsley
3 cups chopped cooked chicken
1½ pounds peeled cooked
  shrimp
½ cup slivered almonds
Sherry to taste

Bake patty shells using package directions. Combine mushrooms and ½ cup chicken broth in saucepan. Cook over low heat until mushrooms are tender. Remove mushrooms with slotted spoon to bowl. Add remaining chicken broth and half and half to saucepan. Stir in flour, salt and pepper until well mixed. Add green onions and parsley. Cook until thickened, stirring constantly. Add chicken, shrimp, almonds and sherry. Heat to serving temperature. Spoon into warm patty shells. **Yield: 10 servings.**

Approx Per Serving: Cal 536; Prot 35 g; Carbo 25 g; Fiber 2 g;
  T Fat 33 g; 56% Calories from Fat; Chol 188 mg; Sod 801 mg.
  Nutritional information does not include sherry.

Wenham Tea House

Chic-à-la-King

1 cup sliced fresh mushrooms
¼ cup chopped green bell
  pepper
2 tablespoons butter
¼ cup butter
¼ cup flour
4 cups half and half
3 cups cubed cooked chicken
1 teaspoon paprika
¼ cup sherry
¼ cup chopped parsley
2 tablespoons chopped canned
  pimentos
Bells seasoning to taste
Salt and pepper to taste

Sauté mushrooms and green pepper in 2 tablespoons butter in skillet. Remove vegetables to plate. Add ¼ cup butter. Cook until melted. Stir in flour until well mixed. Add half and half. Cook over low heat for 5 minutes, stirring constantly. Add vegetables. Cook until thickened, stirring constantly. Add chicken. Cook until heated through, stirring occasionally. Add paprika, sherry and parsley; mix well. Remove from heat. Add pimentos, Bells seasoning, salt and pepper; mix well. Serve over toast, rice or biscuits. **Yield: 8 servings.**

Approx Per Serving: Cal 361; Prot 20 g; Carbo 9 g; Fiber 1 g;
  T Fat 27 g; 68% Calories from Fat; Chol 115 mg; Sod 169 mg.

Wenham Tea House

Chicken Lasagna Casserole

1 8-ounce package lasagna
  noodles
6 ounces cream cheese, softened
1 cup cream-style cottage cheese
⅓ cup chopped onion
⅓ cup chopped celery
⅓ cup sliced stuffed green
  olives
⅓ cup chopped green bell
  pepper
¼ cup finely chopped parsley
1 10-ounce can mushroom
  soup
⅔ cup milk
½ teaspoon salt
½ teaspoon poultry seasoning
3 cups chopped cooked chicken
1½ cups soft bread crumbs
¼ cup melted butter

Cook lasagna noodles using package directions. Rinse in cold water; drain. Combine cream cheese and cottage cheese in bowl; mix well. Add onion, celery, olives, green pepper and parsley; mix well. Mix soup, milk, salt and poultry seasoning in bowl. Layer noodles, cheese mixture, chicken and soup mixture ½ at a time in buttered baking dish. Mix bread crumbs and butter in bowl. Sprinkle over layers. Bake at 375 degrees for 30 minutes. **Yield: 10 servings.**

Approx Per Serving: Cal 354; Prot 21 g; Carbo 25 g; Fiber 1 g;
  T Fat 19 g; 48% Calories from Fat; Chol 74 mg; Sod 729 mg.

Wenham Tea House

Hot Chicken Salad

3 cups cubed cooked chicken
3 cups sliced celery
1¹/₈ cups mayonnaise
1 cup slivered almonds
¹/₂ onion, finely chopped
Lemon juice to taste

1¹/₈ teaspoons MSG
1¹/₈ teaspoons salt
³/₄ cup shredded Cheddar
  cheese
³/₄ cup crushed potato chips

Combine chicken, celery, mayonnaise, almonds, onion, lemon juice, MSG, salt and cheese in bowl; mix well. Spoon into greased casserole; top with crushed potato chips. Bake at 425 degrees for 20 minutes or until hot and bubbly. **Yield: 6 servings.**

Approx Per Serving: Cal 669; Prot 30 g; Carbo 13 g; Fiber 4 g;
    T Fat 57 g; 75% Calories from Fat; Chol 102 mg; Sod 1674 mg.

Wenham Tea House

Scalloped Chicken with Zucchini

¹/₂ cup butter
¹/₂ cup flour
1 teaspoon poultry seasoning
4¹/₂ cups (or more) chicken
  stock
Salt and pepper to taste
1 teaspoon onion powder
1 teaspoon garlic powder

4 cups cubed cooked chicken
3 cups sliced zucchini
1 4-ounce jar sliced pimentos
1 8-ounce can sliced water
  chestnuts
2 3-ounce cans French-fried
  onions

Melt butter in large heavy saucepan. Stir in flour and poultry seasoning until well mixed. Add chicken stock gradually. Cook until thickened, stirring constantly. Add salt, pepper, onion powder, garlic powder, chicken, zucchini, pimentos, water chestnuts and half the French-fried onions, mixing lightly. Add additional chicken stock if necessary for desired consistency. Pour into buttered shallow 12-cup casserole. Bake at 350 degrees for 40 minutes or until zucchini is tender. Sprinkle with remaining French-fried onions. Bake for 5 minutes longer. **Yield: 10 servings.**

Approx Per Serving: Cal 353; Prot 21 g; Carbo 16 g; Fiber 1 g;
    T Fat 22 g; 57% Calories from Fat; Chol 75 mg; Sod 589 mg.

Wenham Tea House

Baked Turkey Croquettes

2/3 cup mayonnaise
11/2 teaspoons Worcestershire
  sauce
1 tablespoon chopped parsley
1 tablespoon lemon juice

1/2 teaspoon salt
Pepper to taste
2 cups cooked rice
3 cups chopped cooked turkey
1 cup fine dry bread crumbs

Combine mayonnaise, Worcestershire sauce, parsley, lemon juice, salt, pepper, rice and turkey in bowl; mix well. Chill, covered, in refrigerator for 30 minutes or longer. Shape into 8 croquettes; roll in bread crumbs to coat. Place in ungreased baking pan. Bake at 450 degrees for 25 minutes or until brown. May substitute chicken or tuna for turkey. **Yield: 8 servings.**

Approx Per Serving: Cal 325; Prot 18 g; Carbo 22 g; Fiber 1 g;
    T Fat 18 g; 50% Calories from Fat; Chol 52 mg; Sod 375 mg.

Wenham Tea House

Topnotch Turkey Loaf

4 cups coarsely ground cooked
  turkey
11/3 cups soft bread crumbs
1 5-ounce can evaporated
  milk
1/3 cup chicken broth
3/4 cup finely chopped celery
2 eggs, beaten

1/3 teaspoon salt
Pepper, nutmeg, rosemary and
  marjoram to taste
1 10-ounce can cream of
  chicken soup
1/3 cup milk
2 tablespoons chopped
  pimento

Combine turkey, bread crumbs, evaported milk, chicken broth, celery, eggs, salt, pepper, nutmeg, rosemary and marjoram in bowl; mix lightly. Line 5x9-inch loaf pan with foil; grease foil. Spoon mixture into pan. Bake at 350 degrees for 45 minutes or until center of loaf is firm. Invert onto serving plate; remove foil. Heat chicken soup, milk and pimento in saucepan until of serving temperature. Pour over turkey loaf. **Yield: 6 servings.**

Approx Per Serving: Cal 301; Prot 34 g; Carbo 12 g; Fiber 1 g;
    T Fat 12 g; 37% Calories from Fat; Chol 155 mg; Sod 715 mg.

Wenham Tea House

Fish au Gratin

4 6-ounce fish filets, cooked
4 hard-boiled eggs, sliced
1/2 green bell pepper, chopped
1 cup Peerless cheese

2 tablespoons mustard sauce
Worcestershire sauce to taste
3/4 cup bread crumbs

Arrange fish in buttered baking dish; top with sliced eggs. Sauté green pepper in nonstick skillet. Melt cheese with mustard sauce and Worcestershire sauce in double boiler, stirring to blend well. Stir in green pepper. Spoon over fish. Top with bread crumbs. Bake at 375 degrees for 30 minutes or until topping is brown. **Yield: 4 servings.**

Approx Per Serving: Cal 444; Prot 48 g; Carbo 17 g; Fiber 1 g;
    T Fat 19 g; 40% Calories from Fat; Chol 339 mg; Sod 563 mg.

Wenham Tea House

Fish Casserole Supreme

1/4 cup chopped onion
1 tablespoon butter
1 10-ounce can Cheddar
    cheese soup
1/2 cup milk
1 10-ounce can cream of
    mushroom soup
1 4-ounce can shrimp,
    drained, rinsed

1 7-ounce can tuna, drained,
    flaked
1/8 teaspoon pepper
6 5 to 6-ounce flounder filets
3 tablespoons flour
1/4 cup fine dry bread crumbs

Sauté onion in butter in electric skillet at medium-low heat, 225 degrees. Mix cheese soup and milk in medium saucepan. Cook over medium-low heat until smooth, stirring to blend well. Stir in mushroom soup; remove from heat. Stir in shrimp, tuna, sautéed onion and pepper. Spoon 1/3 of the sauce into 3-quart baking dish. Coat fish lightly with flour. Arrange in sauce. Top with remaining sauce; sprinkle with bread crumbs. Bake at 350 degrees for 25 minutes or until fish flakes easily. **Yield: 6 servings.**

Approx Per Serving: Cal 392; Prot 52 g; Carbo 15 g; Fiber <1 g;
    T Fat 13 g; 30% Calories from Fat; Chol 164 mg; Sod 1083 mg.

Wenham Tea House

Fish Rolls Florentine

2 10-ounce packages frozen
    chopped spinach, thawed
2 cups cooked rice
1 onion, chopped
1 tablespoon butter
6 flounder filets
Paprika, salt and pepper to taste
4 hard-boiled eggs, chopped

2 tablespoons chopped parsley
2 tablespoons mayonnaise
2 10-ounce cans cream of
    celery soup
1 cup white wine
2 tablespoons grated Parmesan
    cheese

Press spinach to remove moisture. Combine with rice in bowl; mix well. Spread in greased shallow baking dish. Sauté onion in butter in skillet. Sprinkle fish filets with paprika, salt and pepper. Combine eggs, sautéed onion, parsley and mayonnaise in bowl; mix well. Spoon onto 1 end of each fish filet. Roll fish to enclose filling; secure with wooden picks. Arrange over spinach mixture. Combine soup, wine and cheese in bowl; mix well. Spoon over fish rolls. Bake at 400 degrees for 25 to 30 minutes or until fish flakes easily. **Yield: 6 servings.**

Approx Per Serving: Cal 420; Prot 33 g; Carbo 31 g; Fiber 4 g;
    T Fat 16 g; 36% Calories from Fat; Chol 224 mg; Sod 1011 mg.

Wenham Tea House

Baked Haddock

4 6-ounce haddock filets
¼ cup milk
¼ cup mayonnaise
1 cup bread crumbs
¼ cup melted butter
1 teaspoon thyme or lemon thyme

1 to 2 teaspoons fresh parsley
    or parsley flakes
½ teaspoon dill
White wine Worcestershire
    sauce to taste

Arrange fish in milk in baking dish. Spread with mayonnaise. Mix bread crumbs, butter, thyme, parsley and dill in bowl. Sprinkle over fish; sprinkle with Worcestershire sauce. Bake at 350 degrees for 20 to 30 minutes or until fish flakes easily. **Yield: 4 servings.**

Approx Per Serving: Cal 464; Prot 41 g; Carbo 19 g; Fiber 1 g;
    T Fat 26 g; 49% Calories from Fat; Chol 143 mg; Sod 484 mg.

Wenham Tea House

Creole Haddock

2 pounds haddock filets
1½ cups chopped fresh
  tomatoes
½ cup finely chopped green
  bell pepper
⅓ cup lemon juice
1 tablespoon oil

2 teaspoons instant minced
  onion
4 drops of Tabasco sauce
1 teaspoon basil
2 teaspoons salt
¼ teaspoon coarsely ground
  pepper

Arrange fish in single layer in shallow 3-quart baking dish. Combine tomatoes, green pepper, lemon juice, oil, onion, Tabasco sauce, basil, salt and pepper in bowl. Spoon over fish. Bake at 500 degrees for 5 to 8 minutes or until fish flakes easily. Remove to warm serving platter. Garnish with tomato wedges and green pepper rings. **Yield: 6 servings.**

Approx Per Serving: Cal 175; Prot 33 g; Carbo 4 g; Fiber 1 g;
  T Fat 4 g; 18% Calories from Fat; Chol 90 mg; Sod 820 mg.

Wenham Tea House

Scalloped Haddock

½ cup flour
½ cup melted butter
4 cups milk
1 teaspoon mustard

2 cups shredded Cheddar
  cheese
3 pounds haddock, cooked
1 cup bread crumbs

Blend flour into butter in saucepan. Cook until bubbly. Stir in milk and mustard. Cook until thickened, stirring constantly. Stir in cheese until melted. Flake fish into greased baking dish. Spoon sauce over fish; top with crumbs. Bake at 350 degrees just until heated through. May add hard-boiled eggs and sautéed onion and/or green pepper.
Yield: 8 servings.

Approx Per Serving: Cal 525; Prot 50 g; Carbo 21 g; Fiber 1 g;
  T Fat 27 g; 46% Calories from Fat; Chol 179 mg; Sod 542 mg.

Wenham Tea House

Sea Bass with Shrimp

1 pound sea bass steaks
1 tablespoon olive oil
2 medium tomatoes, chopped
1 8-ounce can mushroom
  pieces, drained
3 cloves of garlic, thinly sliced

8 ounces cooked shrimp
1/4 bunch parsley
2 medium tomatoes, cut into
  wedges
1 lemon, cut into wedges

Arrange fish in single layer in shallow baking pan; brush with 1 teaspoon olive oil. Combine remaining olive oil with chopped tomatoes, mushrooms and garlic in bowl; mix well. Spoon over fish. Bake at 400 degrees for 10 minutes per inch of thickness of fish. Sprinkle shrimp over top. Bake for 3 to 4 minutes longer or until fish flakes easily. Remove to parsley-lined platter. Arrange tomato and lemon wedges around fish. **Yield: 5 servings.**

Approx Per Serving: Cal 196; Prot 29 g; Carbo 9 g; Fiber 3 g;
  T Fat 5 g; 25% Calories from Fat; Chol 127 mg; Sod 368 mg.

Mardi Lowery, Chairman, Town Meeting Lunch

Filet of Sole Florentine

2 pounds sole filets
2 tablespoons butter
1/2 teaspoon salt
2 10-ounce packages frozen
  chopped spinach, cooked,
  drained
3 tablespoons sherry

1 10-ounce can cream of
  mushroom soup
3 tablespoons dry bread crumbs
1 tablespoon melted butter
2 tablespoons grated Parmesan
  cheese

Arrange fish in baking dish. Dot with butter; sprinkle with salt. Bake, covered with foil, at 350 degrees for 15 minutes; drain. Spread spinach over fish. Blend sherry and soup in bowl. Spoon over spinach. Top with mixture of bread crumbs, melted butter and cheese. Bake for 20 minutes. **Yield: 6 servings.**

Approx Per Serving: Cal 295; Prot 34 g; Carbo 11 g; Fiber 3 g;
  T Fat 12 g; 38% Calories from Fat; Chol 100 mg; Sod 871 mg.

Wenham Tea House

Filet of Sole Monte Carlo

1   10-ounce package frozen
   chopped spinach, cooked
6 sole filets
1/4 cup grated Parmesan cheese
2 tablespoons flour
2 tablespoons melted butter
1 1/2 cups consommé

Salt and pepper to taste
1/2 cup light cream
1 tablespoon (or more) sherry
2 tablespoons grated Parmesan
   cheese
1 tablespoon butter

Spread spinach in buttered shallow baking dish. Layer fish over spinach; sprinkle with 1/4 cup cheese. Blend flour into melted butter in saucepan. Cook until bubbly. Stir in consommé. Cook for 5 minutes, stirring constantly. Season with salt and pepper. Stir in cream and sherry. Spoon over casserole. Sprinkle with 2 tablespoons cheese; dot with 1 tablespoon butter. Bake at 350 degrees for 30 minutes or until fish flakes easily. Garnish with lemon slices and watercress. Serve with hot cooked rice or noodles. May substitute flounder for sole or broccoli for spinach. May prepare 1 package dry vegetable soup mix using package directions, strain, reserving liquid, and substitute liquid for consommé.
Yield: 6 servings.

Approx Per Serving: Cal 1863; Prot 357 g; Carbo 6 g; Fiber 1 g;
   T Fat 36 g; 18% Calories from Fat; Chol 1032 mg; Sod 2030 mg.

Wenham Tea House

Tuna and Cashew Casserole

1   3-ounce can chow mein
   noodles
1   7-ounce can tuna, drained
1   10-ounce can cream of
   mushroom soup
1/4 cup water

3/4 cup chopped salted cashews
1/3 cup chopped celery
1/4 cup minced onion
1/4 cup chopped black olives
1/2 teaspoon salt
Pepper to taste

Reserve 3/4 cup noodles for topping. Combine remaining noodles with tuna, soup, water, cashews, celery, onion, olives, salt and pepper in bowl; mix well. Spoon into greased 1 1/2-quart baking dish. Sprinkle with reserved noodles. Bake at 350 degrees for 40 minutes. **Yield: 4 servings.**

Approx Per Serving: Cal 404; Prot 23 g; Carbo 26 g; Fiber 3 g;
   T Fat 25 g; 54% Calories from Fat; Chol 31 mg; Sod 1472 mg.

Wenham Tea House

Tuna with Cheese Swirls

2 cups sifted flour
4 teaspoons baking powder
1/2 teaspoon salt
4 teaspoons shortening
2/3 cup milk
3/4 cup shredded American
  cheese
2 tablespoons chopped pimento
Cayenne pepper to taste
1/3 cup chopped green bell
  pepper

3 tablespoons chopped onion
1/4 cup margarine
6 tablespoons flour
1 teaspoon salt
Black pepper to taste
1   10-ounce can chicken with
  rice soup
1 1/2 cups milk
1   7-ounce can white tuna
1 tablespoon lemon juice

Sift flour with baking powder and salt in bowl. Cut in shortening until crumbly. Add milk; mix lightly with fork. Roll into rectangle on lightly floured surface. Sprinkle with shredded cheese, pimento and cayenne pepper. Roll to enclose filling. Cut into slices. Sauté green pepper and onion in margarine in saucepan until tender. Stir in flour, salt and black pepper. Add soup and milk gradually. Cook until thickened, stirring constantly. Stir in tuna and lemon juice. Spoon into baking dish. Top with cheese swirls. Bake at 425 degrees for 25 minutes. May also add pimento to tuna mixture if desired. **Yield: 6 servings.**

Approx Per Serving: Cal 443; Prot 22 g; Carbo 44 g; Fiber 2 g;
  T Fat 19 g; 39% Calories from Fat; Chol 44 mg; Sod 1514 mg.

Wenham Tea House

Seafood au Gratin

3 pounds fish filets
1/4 cup flour
1/4 cup melted butter
2 cups milk
2 cups shredded Cheddar
  cheese

1 teaspoon Worcestershire sauce
1/2 teaspoon salt
Pepper to taste
1/2 cup bread crumbs

Arrange fish in shallow baking dish. Blend flour into butter in saucepan over low heat. Stir in milk. Cook until thickened, stirring constantly. Stir in cheese, Worcestershire sauce, salt and pepper. Cook until cheese melts, stirring to mix well. Spoon over fish. Top with bread crumbs. Bake at 350 degrees for 30 to 35 minutes or until fish flakes easily. May add shrimp and sea legs and season white sauce with garlic powder and onion powder if desired. **Yield: 8 servings.**

Approx Per Serving: Cal 400; Prot 43 g; Carbo 11 g; Fiber <1 g;
  T Fat 20 g; 45% Calories from Fat; Chol 147 mg; Sod 577 mg.

Wenham Tea House

Crab Casserole

6 slices white bread
2 tablespoons butter, softened
1 pound frozen king crab meat,
    thawed
1¹/₂ cups shredded Cheddar
    cheese
3 eggs

¹/₄ teaspoon mustard
¹/₄ cup sherry
2¹/₄ cups milk
Salt and pepper to taste
¹/₂ cup shredded Cheddar
    cheese

Spread untrimmed bread with butter. Cut each slice into 4 strips. Alternate layers of bread, crab meat and 1¹/₂ cups cheese in greased 2-quart baking dish until all ingredients are used. Beat eggs in bowl. Add mustard, sherry, milk, salt and pepper; mix well. Pour over layers. Chill overnight. Sprinkle with ¹/₂ cup cheese. Bake at 350 degrees for 1 hour. **Yield: 6 servings.**

Approx Per Serving: Cal 422; Prot 30 g; Carbo 19 g; Fiber 1 g;
    T Fat 24 g; 53% Calories from Fat; Chol 245 mg; Sod 729 mg.

Wenham Tea House

Crab Meat Tetrazzini

2 10-ounce packages frozen
    broccoli spears
8 ounces uncooked spaghetti
3 cups cheese sauce

2 cups flaked crab meat
8 ounces mushrooms, sliced
¹/₂ cup grated Parmesan cheese

Cook broccoli and spaghetti in separate saucepans using package directions; drain. Layer broccoli and spaghetti in buttered baking dish. Combine cheese sauce with crab meat and mushrooms in bowl; mix well. Spoon over spaghetti; top with Parmesan cheese. Bake at 350 degrees until bubbly. **Yield: 6 servings.**

Approx Per Serving: Cal 460; Prot 28 g; Carbo 44 g; Fiber 5 g;
    T Fat 20 g; 38% Calories from Fat; Chol 81 mg; Sod 689 mg.

Wenham Tea House

Maine Shrimp Casserole

8 slices bread
3 tablespoons butter, softened
8 ounces sharp Cheddar cheese,
  finely chopped
2 cups cooked Maine shrimp
3 eggs

2 1/2 cups milk
Worcestershire sauce and MSG
  to taste
1/2 teaspoon salt
Pepper and paprika to taste

Spread bread with butter; cut into cubes. Alternate layers of bread cubes, cheese and shrimp in buttered baking dish until all ingredients are used. Beat eggs in mixer bowl. Beat in milk, Worcestershire sauce, MSG, salt and pepper. Spoon over layers; sprinkle with paprika. Bake at 350 degrees for 1 hour. May substitute 1 can cream of celery soup for 1 cup milk. **Yield: 4 servings.**

Approx Per Serving: Cal 692; Prot 46 g; Carbo 36 g; Fiber 1 g;
   T Fat 40 g; 52% Calories from Fat; Chol 429 mg; Sod 1285 mg.

Wenham Tea House

Seafood and Rice Casserole

2 cups cooked rice
1/2 cup finely chopped green
  bell pepper
1/2 cup finely chopped celery
1/2 cup finely chopped onion
1 4-ounce can sliced water
  chestnuts, drained
1 cup mayonnaise
1 cup tomato juice

1/4 teaspoon salt
1/8 teaspoon pepper
8 ounces peeled shrimp, cooked
1 7-ounce can king crab meat,
  drained
8 ounces bay scallops
1/4 cup sliced almonds
1 cup shredded Cheddar cheese
Paprika to taste

Combine rice, green pepper, celery, onion and water chestnuts in bowl; mix well. Spread in buttered 2-quart shallow baking dish. Combine mayonnaise, tomato juice, salt and pepper in bowl. Spread half the mixture over casserole. Arrange shrimp, crab meat and scallops around edge of casserole. Drizzle seafood with remaining tomato juice mixture. Sprinkle mixture of almonds and cheese in center of casserole; sprinkle lightly with paprika. Bake, covered, at 350 degrees for 25 to 30 minutes or until bubbly. **Yield: 8 servings.**

Approx Per Serving: Cal 418; Prot 21 g; Carbo 19 g; Fiber 1 g;
   T Fat 29 g; 62% Calories from Fat; Chol 107 mg; Sod 607 mg.

Wenham Tea House

Seafood Lasagna

1 large yellow onion, chopped
4 cloves of garlic, minced
3 tablespoons olive oil
5 cups canned plum tomatoes
   in purée
1/2 cup dry white wine
1/2 cup chopped fresh basil
2 teaspoons fennel seed
Salt and freshly ground pepper
   to taste
1 cup whipping cream
2 tablespoons Pernod
1 pound medium shrimp,
   peeled, lightly poached
1 pound scallops, lightly
   poached
1 pound haddock, lightly
   poached

1 1/4 pounds uncooked fresh
   tomato lasagna noodles
3 cups ricotta cheese
8 ounces cream cheese, softened
2 eggs
1 10-ounce package frozen
   chopped spinach, cooked,
   drained
1 pound cooked lump crab
   meat, shredded
1 bunch scallions, sliced
1 red bell pepper, chopped
1/2 cup chopped fresh basil
1 1/2 pounds mozzarella cheese,
   thinly sliced

Sauté onion and garlic in olive oil in large skillet over medium-high heat for 5 minutes. Add tomatoes. Cook for 5 minutes. Stir in wine, basil, fennel seed, salt and pepper. Simmer for 45 minutes, stirring occasionally. Stir in cream and liqueur. Spread a thin layer of sauce in buttered large rectangular baking dish. Add shrimp, scallops and haddock to remaining sauce. Simmer for 5 minutes longer. Cook noodles *al dente* in boiling salted water in saucepan. Drain and rinse in cool water. Combine ricotta cheese, cream cheese and eggs in bowl; beat with wooden spoon until smooth. Stir in spinach, crab meat, scallions, bell pepper, basil, salt and pepper. Layer 1/3 of the noodles, half the spinach mixture, half the seafood sauce, 1/3 of the mozzarella cheese, half the remaining noodles, all the remaining spinach mixture, half the remaining mozzarella, remaining noodles, remaining seafood sauce and remaining mozzarella cheese in prepared baking dish. Bake at 350 degrees for 50 minutes or until bubbly and brown. Let stand for 10 minutes before serving.
Yield: 12 servings.

Approx Per Serving: Cal 807; Prot 60 g; Carbo 47 g; Fiber 4 g;
   T Fat 41 g; 47% Calories from Fat; Chol 333 mg; Sod 657 mg.

Wenham Tea House

Deviled Eggs with Cheese-Shrimp Sauce

9 hard-boiled eggs
3 tablespoons mayonnaise
1 tablespoon chopped sweet
  pickle
2 teaspoons vinegar
1/2 teaspoon dry mustard
Worcestershire sauce and
  pepper to taste

4 cups hot cooked rice
1 10-ounce can Cheddar
   cheese soup
3/4 cup milk
1 4-ounce can mushroom
   pieces, drained
1 4-ounce can shrimp, rinsed,
   drained

Cut eggs into halves lengthwise. Remove yolks to bowl and mash with fork. Add mayonnaise, pickle, vinegar, dry mustard, Worcestershire sauce and pepper; mix well. Spoon into egg whites, heaping slightly. Spread rice in ungreased 8x12-inch baking dish. Arrange eggs in 3 rows on rice. Bring soup, milk, mushrooms and shrimp to a boil in saucepan, stirring occasionally. Spoon over eggs. Bake at 350 degrees for 15 minutes or until heated through. **Yield: 9 servings.**

Approx Per Serving: Cal 282; Prot 13 g; Carbo 28 g; Fiber 1 g;
   T Fat 13 g; 41% Calories from Fat; Chol 248 mg; Sod 421 mg.

Wenham Tea House

Artichoke Frittata

2 6-ounce jars marinated
   artichokes
1 onion, finely chopped
5 eggs

2 1/2 ounces Cheddar cheese,
   shredded
2 1/2 ounces Monterey Jack
   cheese, shredded

Drain artichokes, reserving marinade from 1 jar; chop artichokes. Sauté onion in reserved marinade in skillet until tender. Beat eggs in mixer bowl. Add cheeses, artichokes and sautéed onion; mix well. Spoon into buttered 8x8-inch baking dish. Bake at 375 degrees for 30 to 45 minutes or until set in center and light brown on edges. May cut into small squares to serve as appetizers. **Yield: 8 servings.**

Approx Per Serving: Cal 167; Prot 9 g; Carbo 5 g; Fiber 3 g;
   T Fat 13 g; 66% Calories from Fat; Chol 151 mg; Sod 371 mg.

Lesley Blanchette, Chairman, Tea House

Mock Cheese Soufflé

8 slices bread
8 ounces Swiss cheese,
 shredded
4 ounces Cheddar cheese,
 shredded
1/2 cup melted butter
3 or 4 eggs

2 1/2 cups milk
1/2 to 1 teaspoon mustard
1/2 teaspoon salt
1/2 teaspoon pepper or white
 pepper
Paprika to taste

Trim crusts from bread and cut slices into cubes. Reserve a small amount of cheeses for topping. Layer half the bread in buttered 9x13-inch baking dish. Drizzle with melted butter; sprinkle with half the remaining cheeses. Repeat layers. Beat eggs in bowl. Add milk, mustard, salt and pepper; mix well. Spoon over layers. Sprinkle with reserved cheeses and paprika. Chill for 45 minutes to overnight. Bake at 350 degrees for 50 minutes. May substitute Tybo, Havarti or Gruyère cheese for Swiss cheese. **Yield: 6 servings.**

Approx Per Serving: Cal 570; Prot 26 g; Carbo 25 g; Fiber 1 g;
 T Fat 41 g; 64% Calories from Fat; Chol 252 mg; Sod 814 mg.

Bonnie B. Rollins, Exchange Book Shop

Quiche Lorraine

12 slices bacon, crisp-fried,
 crumbled
1 cup shredded Swiss cheese
1/2 cup minced onion
1 unbaked 9-inch pie shell
4 eggs

2 cups light cream
1/4 teaspoon sugar
1/8 teaspoon nutmeg
3/4 teaspoon salt
Black pepper to taste
1/8 teaspoon cayenne pepper

Sprinkle bacon, cheese and onion in pie shell. Combine eggs, cream, sugar, nutmeg, salt, black pepper and cayenne pepper in bowl; beat with rotary beater until smooth. Pour into prepared pie shell. Bake at 425 degrees for 15 minutes. Reduce oven temperature to 300 degrees. Bake for 30 minutes longer or until knife inserted 1 inch from edge comes out clean. Let stand for 10 minutes before serving. **Yield: 6 servings.**

Approx Per Serving: Cal 585; Prot 17 g; Carbo 18 g; Fiber 1 g;
 T Fat 50 g; 76% Calories from Fat; Chol 258 mg; Sod 775 mg.

Wenham Tea House

Onion Pie

2 large red or yellow onions,
 sliced
1 tablespoon butter
3 tablespoons flour
1/2 cup light cream

3/4 teaspoon salt
1/2 teaspoon pepper
2 eggs, beaten
1 unbaked 8-inch pie shell

Sauté onions in butter in skillet until tender. Sprinkle with flour; remove from heat. Add cream, salt and pepper. Stir in eggs. Spoon into pie shell. Bake at 400 degrees for 45 minutes. May add spinach or bell peppers if desired. **Yield: 8 servings.**

Approx Per Serving: Cal 213; Prot 4 g; Carbo 16 g; Fiber 1 g;
 T Fat 15 g; 63% Calories from Fat; Chol 74 mg; Sod 373 mg.

Wenham Tea House

Spinach Pie

1 10-ounce package frozen
 chopped spinach, thawed
1/2 zucchini, chopped
1/2 green bell pepper, chopped
4 ounces mushrooms, chopped
2 tablespoons oil
4 eggs

2 pounds ricotta cheese
1 cup shredded mozzarella
 cheese
1 tablespoon garlic powder
1 teaspoon salt
1/2 teaspoon pepper
2 tablespoons margarine

Sauté spinach, zucchini, green pepper and mushrooms in oil in skillet. Beat eggs with ricotta cheese, mozzarella cheese, garlic powder, salt and pepper in bowl. Add sautéed vegetables; mix well. Spoon into greased 9x13-inch baking pan. Dot with margarine. Bake at 350 degrees for 40 minutes. **Yield: 8 servings.**

Approx Per Serving: Cal 348; Prot 20 g; Carbo 7 g; Fiber 1 g;
 T Fat 27 g; 69% Calories from Fat; Chol 175 mg; Sod 514 mg.

Wenham Tea House

Tea House Spinach Pie

1 10-ounce package frozen
   chopped spinach, thawed,
   drained
12 ounces cottage cheese
1 cup shredded Cheddar cheese

3 eggs
2 tablespoons oil
1 teaspoon crushed garlic
1/8 teaspoon nutmeg

Combine spinach, cottage cheese, Cheddar cheese, eggs, oil, garlic and nutmeg in bowl; mix well. Spoon into lightly oiled 9-inch pie plate. Bake at 350 degrees for 40 minutes or until knife inserted near center comes out clean and top is light brown. **Yield: 8 servings.**

Approx Per Serving: Cal 171; Prot 12 g; Carbo 4 g; Fiber 1 g;
   T Fat 12 g; 63% Calories from Fat; Chol 101 mg; Sod 316 mg.

Wenham Tea House

Zucchini Quiche

6 eggs
1 unbaked 9-inch pie shell
1 1/4 cups milk
1 1/4 teaspoons tarragon
1/2 teaspoon celery seed
1/2 teaspoon salt

1/4 teaspoon pepper
2 cups sliced zucchini
1/2 onion, chopped
2 tablespoons margarine
1/2 cup grated Parmesan cheese

Beat eggs in mixer bowl. Brush a small amount of beaten egg into pie shell. Add milk, tarragon, celery seed, salt and pepper to remaining eggs; beat until smooth. Sauté zucchini and onion in margarine in skillet until tender but not brown. Spoon into prepared pie shell. Sprinkle with Parmesan cheese. Pour egg mixture over top. Bake at 450 degrees for 5 minutes. Reduce oven temperature to 375 degrees. Bake for 30 to 40 minutes longer or until set. **Yield: 6 servings.**

Approx Per Serving: Cal 336; Prot 13 g; Carbo 19 g; Fiber 1 g;
   T Fat 23 g; 62% Calories from Fat; Chol 225 mg; Sod 623 mg.

Wenham Tea House

Hobbs House

Vegetables and Side Dishes

Green Beans Oriental

2 10-ounce packages frozen
  French-style green beans
Salt to taste
1 19-ounce can bean sprouts,
  drained
1 5-ounce can sliced water
  chestnuts, drained
1/2 cup grated Parmesan cheese
4 tablespoons butter

2 tablespoons flour
1/4 teaspoon black pepper
Cayenne pepper to taste
1/4 teaspoon Worcestershire
  sauce
2 cups heavy cream
1 cup finely chopped
  unblanched almonds
2 tablespoons butter

Cook beans in boiling salted water in saucepan for 5 minutes; drain. Alternate layers of beans, bean sprouts, water chestnuts and cheese in shallow 2-quart casserole. Melt 4 tablespoons butter in saucepan. Add flour, salt, black pepper, cayenne pepper and Worcestershire sauce, stirring until blended. Stir in cream slowly. Cook over medium heat until thickened, stirring constantly. Pour over layered vegetables, lifting with fork to coat. Sauté almonds in 2 tablespoons butter. Sprinkle over top layer. Bake at 425 degrees for 15 to 20 minutes or until heated through and almonds are brown. **Yield: 8 servings.**

Approx Per Serving: Cal 444; Prot 9 g; Carbo 15 g; Fiber 6 g;
  T Fat 41 g; 80% Calories from Fat; Chol 109 mg; Sod 210 mg.

Wenham Tea House

Broccoli with Sour Cream Sauce

2 10-ounce packages frozen
  broccoli
2 tablespoons butter
2 tablespoons minced onion
2 teaspoons sugar

1 teaspoon vinegar
1/8 teaspoon pepper
1 1/2 cups sour cream
1/4 cup chopped pecans

Cook broccoli using package directions; drain. Melt butter in top of double boiler. Add onion. Cook until tender. Add sugar, vinegar and pepper; mix well. Stir in sour cream slowly. Cook over warm water until heated through, stirring constantly. Serve over broccoli. Sprinkle with chopped pecans. May substitute squash or other vegetables for broccoli. **Yield: 6 servings.**

Approx Per Serving: Cal 223; Prot 5 g; Carbo 10 g; Fiber 3 g;
  T Fat 19 g; 74% Calories from Fat; Chol 36 mg; Sod 86 mg.

Wenham Tea House

Sprouts Emerald Isle

10 ounces cream cheese
2 cups milk
2½ tablespoons sherry
2½ teaspoons parsley flakes
3¾ teaspoons onion salt

¾ teaspoon salt
1½ cups water
2½ 10-ounce packages frozen
  Brussels sprouts, thawed
¾ cup bread crumbs

Heat cream cheese and milk in saucepan over low heat, stirring until smooth. Add sherry, parsley and onion salt; mix well. Pour half the sauce into a 6-inch baking dish. Cook Brussels sprouts in salted water in saucepan for 4 minutes; drain. Arrange over sauce. Cover with remaining sauce; sprinkle with bread crumbs. Bake at 325 degrees for 30 minutes. **Yield: 10 servings.**

Approx Per Serving: Cal 194; Prot 7 g; Carbo 15 g; Fiber 3 g;
  T Fat 12 g; 55% Calories from Fat; Chol 38 mg; Sod 1105 mg.

Wenham Tea House

Cauliflower and Mushroom Casserole

Flowerets of 1 large head
  cauliflower
3 quarts water
½ teaspoon salt
1 onion, chopped
¼ cup butter
16 ounces fresh mushrooms,
  sliced

¼ cup butter
3 tablespoons flour
½ teaspoon salt
⅛ teaspoon pepper
⅛ teaspoon paprika
1½ cups milk
½ cup bread crumbs
1 teaspoon melted butter

Cook cauliflowerets in boiling salted water until tender; drain. Arrange in baking dish. Sauté onion in ¼ cup butter in saucepan until light brown. Add mushrooms. Sauté until tender; set aside. Melt ¼ cup butter in same saucepan. Add flour, ½ teaspoon salt, pepper and paprika, stirring until blended. Add milk. Cook until thickened, stirring constantly. Stir in mushrooms. Pour mixture over cauliflowerets. Toss bread crumbs with melted butter; sprinkle over cauliflowerets. Bake at 350 degrees for 25 minutes. **Yield: 4 servings.**

Approx Per Serving: Cal 404; Prot 10 g; Carbo 31 g; Fiber 6 g;
  T Fat 29 g; 61% Calories from Fat; Chol 78 mg; Sod 884 mg.

Wenham Tea House

Corn Casserole

1 17-ounce can cream-style
  corn
2 egg yolks, beaten
1/8 teaspoon pepper
1 teaspoon salt

1 tablespoon sugar
2 tablespoons milk
3 tablespoons melted butter
2 egg whites

Combine corn, egg yolks, pepper, salt, sugar, milk and butter in 1½-quart casserole. Beat egg whites in mixer bowl until stiff peaks form. Fold into corn mixture. Place casserole in *bain-marie* (pan filled with water). Bake at 350 degrees on lowest rack in oven for 1 hour. **Yield: 4 servings.**

Approx Per Serving: Cal 220; Prot 6 g; Carbo 26 g; Fiber 3 g;
   T Fat 12 g; 47% Calories from Fat; Chol 131 mg; Sod 981 mg.

Wenham Tea House

Eggplant and Mushroom Casserole

1 large eggplant, peeled, cut
  into 1-inch slices
1/2 teaspoon salt
4 large onions, sliced
1 or 2 cloves of garlic, chopped
1/4 cup butter
12 ounces fresh mushrooms
4 large tomatoes, peeled,
  chopped
2 green bell peppers, cut into
  julienne strips

2 teaspoons salt
1 teaspoon freshly ground
  pepper
1 bay leaf
1/4 teaspoon basil
1/4 teaspoon oregano
1/8 teaspoon ground cloves
1 cup dry bread crumbs
1/4 cup melted butter

Place eggplant in saucepan. Add boiling water to cover; add 1/2 teaspoon salt. Reduce heat. Simmer for 10 minutes; drain. Sauté onions and garlic in 1/4 cup butter in skillet until light brown. Remove and discard stems from mushrooms. Add mushroom caps to onion mixture. Sauté for 5 minutes. Add tomatoes, green peppers, 2 teaspoons salt, pepper, bay leaf, basil, oregano and cloves. Simmer for 10 minutes, stirring occasionally. Remove bay leaf. Alternate layers of eggplant and vegetable mixture in 2-quart casserole. Toss bread crumbs with melted butter. Sprinkle over top of vegetables. Bake at 275 degrees for 1½ hours. **Yield: 8 servings.**

Approx Per Serving: Cal 214; Prot 5 g; Carbo 23 g; Fiber 5 g;
   T Fat 13 g; 51% Calories from Fat; Chol 32 mg; Sod 865 mg.

Lillian M. Sweenie, Wenham Exchange

Baked Mushrooms

1 10-ounce package frozen
   spinach soufflé

24 medium mushroom caps
1/3 cup grated Parmesan cheese

Thaw spinach soufflé. Spoon into mushroom caps. Arrange on baking sheet. Sprinkle with Parmesan cheese. Bake at 400 degrees for 15 minutes. Serve hot. **Yield: 6 servings.**

Approx Per Serving: Cal 110; Prot 7 g; Carbo 4 g; Fiber 2 g;
   T Fat 8 g; 63% Calories from Fat; Chol 67 mg; Sod 350 mg.

Georgette Hewson, Wenham Exchange

French Onion Casserole

8 large Vidalia onions
3 tablespoons butter
1 10-ounce can cream of
   chicken soup

1 soup can milk
8 ounces Swiss cheese, sliced
15 slices French bread
1 tablespoon butter

Slice onions 1/4 inch thick; separate into rings. Sauté in 3 tablespoons butter in skillet until tender. Arrange in 9x13-inch baking dish. Pour mixture of soup and milk over onions. Layer with cheese slices. Spread bread with 1 tablespoon butter. Arrange over top. Bake at 350 degrees for 20 to 30 minutes or until brown. **Yield: 12 servings.**

Approx Per Serving: Cal 303; Prot 12 g; Carbo 33 g; Fiber 3 g;
   T Fat 13 g; 39% Calories from Fat; Chol 33 mg; Sod 533 mg.

Jacqueline Rabot, Tea House Staff

Country Potato Casserole

1/2 cup melted margarine
1 10-ounce can cream of
   mushroom soup
1 10-ounce can cream of
   chicken soup
1 cup sour cream
1/2 cup chopped scallions

2 cups shredded sharp Cheddar
   cheese
Salt and pepper to taste
1 2-pound package frozen
   hashed brown potatoes, thawed
2 tablespoons melted margarine
1 cup cornflake crumbs

Combine first 8 ingredients in bowl; mix well. Add potatoes, stirring to coat. Pour into greased 9x13-inch baking pan. Top with mixture of 2 tablespoons margarine and cornflake crumbs. Bake at 350 degrees for 45 minutes. **Yield: 16 servings.**

Approx Per Serving: Cal 327; Prot 7 g; Carbo 23 g; Fiber 1 g;
   T Fat 24 g; 64% Calories from Fat; Chol 23 mg; Sod 534 mg.

Wenham Tea House

Creamy Potato Puff

4 cups hot mashed potatoes
8 ounces cream cheese, softened
1/3 cup chopped onion
1 egg, beaten

1 2-ounce jar chopped
   pimento, drained
1 teaspoon salt

Combine all ingredients in bowl; mix well. Spoon into baking dish. Bake at 350 degrees for 45 minutes. **Yield: 6 servings.**

Approx Per Serving: Cal 258; Prot 7 g; Carbo 27 g; Fiber 2 g;
     T Fat 15 g; 50% Calories from Fat; Chol 79 mg; Sod 903 mg.

Deborah McClelland, WVIS Member and Volunteer

Party Potatoes

8 ounces cream cheese, softened
1 cup sour cream
8 to 10 potatoes, peeled,
   cooked, mashed
3 tablespoons chopped chives

Salt, pepper and garlic salt to
   taste
1/4 cup butter
1 cup shredded Cheddar cheese

Beat cream cheese and sour cream in mixer bowl until light and fluffy. Fold in mashed potatoes, chives, salt, pepper and garlic salt. Spoon into greased baking dish. Dot with butter; sprinkle with cheese. Bake at 325 degrees for 1 hour. **Yield: 10 servings.**

Approx Per Serving: Cal 360; Prot 8 g; Carbo 35 g; Fiber 2 g;
     T Fat 21 g; 52% Calories from Fat; Chol 59 mg; Sod 196 mg.

Wenham Tea House

Do-Ahead Mashed Potatoes

10 medium potatoes, peeled
2 3-ounce packages cream
   cheese, softened
1 cup sour cream

2 teaspoons onion salt
1/4 teaspoon freshly ground
   pepper
2 tablespoons butter, softened

Cook potatoes in boiling water in saucepan; drain. Mash in bowl until smooth. Beat in cream cheese, sour cream, onion salt, pepper and butter. Spoon into greased baking dish. Let stand in refrigerator overnight. Bake at 350 degrees for 20 minutes or until heated through. May add milk for smoother mixture. Garnish with shredded cheese. **Yield: 8 servings.**

Approx Per Serving: Cal 343; Prot 6 g; Carbo 44 g; Fiber 3 g;
     T Fat 17 g; 42% Calories from Fat; Chol 44 mg; Sod 625 mg.

Virginia Birkemose, Hobbs House Staff

Refrigerator Mashed Potatoes

5 pounds potatoes, peeled
2 3-ounce packages cream
  cheese with chives, softened
2 teaspoons onion salt
1/4 teaspoon pepper
1/2 cup butter, softened
2 cups sour cream

Cook potatoes in boiling water in saucepan; drain. Mash in bowl until smooth. Beat in cream cheese, onion salt, pepper, butter and sour cream until smooth and fluffy. Bake at 350 degrees for 30 minutes or until heated through. May store in refrigerator before baking for up to 2 weeks. **Yield: 10 servings.**

Approx Per Serving: Cal 451; Prot 7 g; Carbo 52 g; Fiber 3 g;
    T Fat 25 g; 49% Calories from Fat; Chol 64 mg; Sod 574 mg.

Wenham Tea House

Tomato Pie

2 cups Bisquick baking mix
2/3 cup milk
3 or 4 tomatoes, peeled, thinly
  sliced
1/3 cup fresh chopped basil
2 tablespoons chopped chives
1/4 cup chopped onion
Salt and pepper to taste
1 cup shredded sharp Cheddar
  cheese
1 cup mayonnaise

Combine baking mix and milk in small bowl; mix well. Press into greased 9-inch pie plate. Layer half the tomatoes over pastry. Sprinkle with basil, chives, onion, salt and pepper. Place remaining tomatoes over top. Combine cheese and mayonnaise in bowl; mix well. Spread over tomato layer. Bake at 400 degrees for 30 minutes. **Yield: 6 servings.**

Approx Per Serving: Cal 560; Prot 10 g; Carbo 36 g; Fiber 2 g;
    T Fat 43 g; 68% Calories from Fat; Chol 45 mg; Sod 873 mg.

Gail Burnham, Tea House Staff

*Serve **Lemon-Chive Sauce** over potatoes, asparagus, broccoli or carrots. Combine 2/3 cup melted butter, 1/4 cup minced chives, 2 tablespoons lemon juice, 2 teaspoons grated lemon rind, 1 teaspoon salt and pepper to taste.*

Tomato-Zucchini Scallop

2 small zucchini, sliced
1 onion, thinly sliced
2 small tomatoes, peeled, sliced
1 cup plain croutons
1 teaspoon salt

Pepper to taste
1 tomato, cut into wedges
1 cup shredded sharp Cheddar
  cheese

Layer zucchini, onion, tomatoes and croutons ½ at a time in 1½-quart casserole. Season with salt and pepper. Top with tomato wedges. Bake, covered, at 350 degrees for 1 hour. Sprinkle with cheese. Bake, uncovered, for 5 to 10 minutes or until cheese is melted. **Yield: 6 servings.**

Approx Per Serving: Cal 118; Prot 6 g; Carbo 9 g; Fiber 2 g;
    T Fat 7 g; 49% Calories from Fat; Chol 20 mg; Sod 544 mg.

Wenham Tea House

Turnip Casserole from Finland

2 cups cooked, mashed yellow
  turnips
1½ tablespoons sugar
⅛ teaspoon pepper

2 eggs, well beaten
1 teaspoon salt
1 cup soft bread crumbs
3 tablespoons butter

Combine turnips, sugar, pepper, eggs, salt and ¾ cup bread crumbs in bowl; mix well. Pour into buttered 1-quart baking dish. Sprinkle with remaining bread crumbs; dot with butter. Bake at 350 degrees for 20 to 25 minutes or until brown. **Yield: 6 servings.**

Approx Per Serving: Cal 128; Prot 3 g; Carbo 12 g; Fiber 2 g;
    T Fat 8 g; 54% Calories from Fat; Chol 87 mg; Sod 517 mg.

Wenham Tea House

*Make a Sauce for Fresh Zucchini of ¼ cup melted butter,
1 tablespoon grated lemon rind, 2 tablespoons lemon
juice and 2 tablespoons minced onion.*

Curried Fruit

1 20-ounce can chunk
   pineapple, drained
1 16-ounce can sliced pears,
   drained
1 16-ounce can sliced peaches,
   drained

³/₄ cup packed brown sugar
1 tablespoon cornstarch
1 tablespoon curry powder
¹/₂ cup melted butter

Combine pineapple, pears and peaches in 1-quart baking dish. Mix brown sugar, cornstarch, curry powder and melted butter in small bowl. Pour over fruit. Bake at 325 degrees for 1 hour. **Yield: 6 servings.**

Approx Per Serving: Cal 379; Prot 1 g; Carbo 64 g; Fiber 3 g;
   T Fat 16 g; 35% Calories from Fat; Chol 41 mg; Sod 151 mg.

Wenham Tea House

Scalloped Pineapple

¹/₂ cup butter, softened
1 cup sugar
2 eggs, well beaten
1 20-ounce can crushed
   pineapple

3 cups firmly packed bread
   cubes
1 cup miniature marshmallows

Cream butter and sugar in mixer bowl until light and fluffy. Add **eggs;** beat well. Stir in undrained pineapple, bread cubes and marshmallows. Pour into greased 1¹/₂-quart casserole. Bake at 350 degrees for 45 minutes. **Yield: 8 servings.**

Approx Per Serving: Cal 333; Prot 3 g; Carbo 52 g; Fiber 1 g;
   T Fat 14 g; 36% Calories from Fat; Chol 84 mg; Sod 194 mg.

Mrs. F.D. Kuemmerle, Chairman, Program Committee

Baked Rice

1 small onion, chopped
2 stalks celery, chopped
1/2 green bell pepper, chopped
1 tablespoon butter
1 cup uncooked rice

1   10-ounce can beef consommé
1/2 consommé can water
1   7-ounce can mushrooms,
    drained
Steak sauce to taste

Sauté onion, celery and green pepper in butter in saucepan. Add rice, consommé, water, mushrooms and steak sauce; mix well. Spoon into 1½-quart baking dish. Bake at 350 degrees for 1 hour and 10 minutes. **Yield: 6 servings.**

Approx Per Serving: Cal 158; Prot 5 g; Carbo 29 g; Fiber 2 g;
    T Fat 2 g; 13% Calories from Fat; Chol 5 mg; Sod 416 mg.

Wenham Tea House

Orange Rice

1 cup orange juice
1 cup chicken bouillon
1 teaspoon salt
1 teaspoon butter

2 tablespoons chopped green
    onions
1 cup uncooked rice

Combine orange juice, bouillon, salt, butter and green onions in saucepan. Bring to a boil. Stir in rice; reduce heat to low. Steam rice, covered, for 20 to 25 minutes or until liquid is absorbed. **Yield: 4 servings.**

Approx Per Serving: Cal 214; Prot 5 g; Carbo 44 g; Fiber 1 g;
    T Fat 2 g; 7% Calories from Fat; Chol 3 mg; Sod 738 mg.

Wenham Tea House

Rice Pilaf

1 onion, minced
3 tablespoons butter
1 cup uncooked rice
2 cups beef or chicken bouillon

3 slices bacon, crisp-fried,
    crumbled
1/2 cup toasted slivered almonds

Sauté onion in butter in skillet until tender. Add rice. Sauté until pale yellow. Pour into buttered 9x13-inch casserole. Stir in bouillon, bacon and almonds. Bake, covered, at 350 degrees for 1 hour. **Yield: 4 servings.**

Approx Per Serving: Cal 392; Prot 10 g; Carbo 44 g; Fiber 3 g;
    T Fat 20 g; 46% Calories from Fat; Chol 28 mg; Sod 544 mg.

Shirley H. Anderson, Retired Business Director

Spinach-Rice Casserole

1 10-ounce package frozen
   chopped spinach, thawed,
   drained
1 cup cooked rice
1 cup shredded Cheddar cheese
2 eggs, slightly beaten
2 teaspoons butter, softened

⅓ cup milk
2 tablespoons chopped onion
¼ teaspoon Worcestershire
   sauce
1 teaspoon salt
¼ teaspoon crushed rosemary

Combine spinach, rice, cheese, eggs, butter, milk, onion, Worcestershire sauce, salt and rosemary in bowl; mix well. Pour into 9x12-inch baking dish. Bake at 350 degrees for 25 minutes or until set and light brown. **Yield: 6 servings.**

Approx Per Serving: Cal 173; Prot 9 g; Carbo 12 g; Fiber 1 g;
   T Fat 10 g; 51% Calories from Fat; Chol 96 mg; Sod 554 mg.

Wenham Tea House

Vegetable-Rice Casserole

2 cups cooked long grain rice
1 10-ounce package frozen
   tiny peas, thawed
1 cup sour cream
1 cup chopped celery

¼ cup minced onion
1 teaspoon curry powder
½ teaspoon salt
½ teaspoon dry mustard

Combine rice, peas, sour cream, celery, onion, curry powder, salt and mustard in bowl; mix well. Spoon into buttered 1-quart baking dish. Bake at 350 degrees for 25 minutes or until heated through. Serve hot or cold. **Yield: 12 servings.**

Approx Per Serving: Cal 91; Prot 3 g; Carbo 11 g; Fiber 1 g;
   T Fat 4 g; 41% Calories from Fat; Chol 9 mg; Sod 135 mg.

Maggie Birkemose, WVIS Member

*To make **Mushroom Sauce**, sauté ¼ cup chopped green onions in
½ cup butter in saucepan. Add 8 ounces chopped mushrooms and cook
until liquid evaporates. Stir in ½ cup flour, 1½ cups milk, 1½ cups
chicken broth and 2 cups cream. Cook until thickened and smooth, stirring
constantly. Stir in a mixture of 1 cup Swiss cheese, 1 cup
Parmesan cheese, salt and pepper.*

Gnocchi

3 cups milk
6 ounces farina
1¹/₂ teaspoons salt
1¹/₂ cups shredded American
  cheese

2 tablespoons butter
3 egg yolks, beaten
3 egg whites
¹/₂ cup grated Parmesan cheese

Scald milk in double boiler. Stir in farina gradually; add salt. Cook, covered, over low heat for 20 minutes. Remove from heat. Add American cheese, butter and egg yolks; mix well. Beat egg whites in mixer bowl until stiff peaks form. Fold into farina mixture. Spoon into individual buttered baking dishes. Sprinkle with Parmesan cheese. Bake at 375 degrees for 25 to 30 minutes or until brown. **Yield: 6 servings.**

Approx Per Serving: Cal 387; Prot 19 g; Carbo 29 g; Fiber 0 g;
    T Fat 22 g; 51% Calories from Fat; Chol 166 mg; Sod 1177 mg.

Wenham Tea House

Macaroni Supreme

1 cup cooked macaroni
1 cup shredded Cheddar cheese
1 cup soft bread crumbs
1 cup scalded milk
¹/₄ cup chopped green bell
  pepper

¹/₄ cup melted butter
2 ounces chopped pimento
1 teaspoon parsley
3 egg yolks, beaten
3 egg whites

Combine macaroni, cheese, bread crumbs, milk, green pepper, butter, pimento, parsley and egg yolks in large bowl; mix well. Beat egg whites in mixer bowl until stiff peaks form. Fold into macaroni mixture. Pour into greased casserole; place in *bain-marie* (pan filled with water). Bake at 350 degrees for 1 hour. **Yield: 4 servings.**

Approx Per Serving: Cal 386; Prot 16 g; Carbo 18 g; Fiber 1 g;
    T Fat 28 g; 65% Calories from Fat; Chol 229 mg; Sod 399 mg.

Wenham Tea House

*Make an easy **Sweet and Sour Sauce** of ¹/₂ cup pineapple juice,
3 tablespoons oil, 2 tablespoons brown sugar, 1 tablespoon soy sauce,
¹/₄ cup vinegar and ¹/₂ teaspoon pepper.*

Green Tomato Relish

8 quarts green tomatoes
1 cup salt
1 head green cabbage
6 onions
6 green bell peppers
5 red bell peppers

3 quarts cider vinegar
8 cups sugar
2 tablespoons celery seed
2 tablespoons mustard seed
1 tablespoon whole cloves

Place tomatoes a few at a time in food processor container or grinder. Process until finely chopped or ground. Combine with salt. Place in cloth bag; drain overnight. Process cabbage, onions and red and green peppers until finely chopped or ground. Combine with tomatoes in large kettle. Add vinegar, sugar, celery seed, mustard seed and cloves; mix well. Bring to a boil. Cook for 20 minutes, stirring occasionally. Ladle into 16 hot sterilized 1-pint jars, leaving 1/2 inch headspace. Seal with 2-piece lids. **Yield: 256 (2-ounce) servings.**

Approx Per Serving: Cal 34; Prot <1 g; Carbo 9 g; Fiber <1 g;
    T Fat <1 g; 3% Calories from Fat; Chol 0 mg; Sod 403 mg.

Betty Johnson, Past President, WVIS

Epicurean Sauce

3 cups mayonnaise
1 cup whipped cream
1 5-ounce jar prepared
  horseradish

Tabasco sauce to taste
Worcestershire sauce to taste

Combine mayonnaise, whipped cream, horseradish, Tabasco sauce and Worcestershire sauce in bowl; mix well. Store in refrigerator until needed. **Yield: 37 (1-ounce) servings.**

Approx Per Serving: Cal 140; Prot <1 g; Carbo 1 g; Fiber <1 g;
    T Fat 15 g; 97% Calories from Fat; Chol 15 mg; Sod 106 mg.

Wenham Tea House

*For **Creole Sauce**, sauté 1/2 cup chopped onion, 1/4 chopped green pepper and 1 clove of garlic in 2 tablespoons oil. Add one 28-ounce can tomatoes, 1 tablespoon chopped parsley, 2 teaspoons sugar, 1/2 teaspoon chili powder and 1 teaspoon each celery seed, salt and crushed bay leaf.*

Newburg Sauce

1/3 cup butter
2 tablespoons flour
2 cups light cream
4 egg yolks, beaten

1/4 cup sherry
2 teaspoons lemon juice
1/2 teaspoon salt

Melt butter in saucepan. Stir in flour until blended. Add cream gradually, stirring constantly. Cook until thickened, stirring constantly. Remove from heat. Stir a small amount of cream mixture into egg yolks. Stir egg yolks into cream mixture gradually. Cook over low heat until blended, stirring constantly. Add sherry, lemon juice and salt; mix well. **Yield: 7 (1/4-cup) servings.**

Approx Per Serving: Cal 331; Prot 3 g; Carbo 4 g; Fiber <1 g;
    T Fat 33 g; 91% Calories from Fat; Chol 221 mg; Sod 254 mg.

Wenham Tea House

Raisin Sauce for Ham

1 cup packed brown sugar
2 tablespoons cornstarch
1 cup water

1/4 cup vinegar
1/4 cup raisins

Combine brown sugar and cornstarch in saucepan. Add water, vinegar and raisins; mix well. Cook over medium heat until thickened, stirring constantly. Serve over ham slices. **Yield: 5 (1/4-cup) servings.**

Approx Per Serving: Cal 243; Prot <1 g; Carbo 63 g; Fiber 1 g;
    T Fat <1 g; 0% Calories from Fat; Chol 0 mg; Sod 25 mg.

Wenham Tea House

Apricot Glaze for Ham

1 cup packed brown sugar
2 tablespoons cornstarch
1   24-ounce can apricot nectar

2 tablespoons lemon juice
1 teaspoon ginger
1/2 teaspoon salt

Combine brown sugar, cornstarch, apricot nectar, lemon juice, ginger and salt in saucepan; mix well. Cook over medium heat until thickened, stirring constantly. Brush on ham during last 30 minutes of cooking time. **Yield: 12 servings.**

Approx Per Serving: Cal 123; Prot <1 g; Carbo 32 g; Fiber <1 g;
    T Fat 1 g; 0% Calories from Fat; Chol 0 mg; Sod 101 mg.

Wenham Tea House

Main St. Barn

Breads

Fluffy Biscuits

3³/₄ cups flour
4 teaspoons baking powder
2 teaspoons salt

6 tablespoons margarine
1¹/₂ cups light cream

Combine flour, baking powder and salt in bowl; mix well. Cut in margarine until mixture is crumbly. Stir in cream until well mixed. Roll out on lightly floured surface. Cut with 2-inch biscuit cutter. Arrange on baking sheet. Bake at 425 degrees for 12 to 15 minutes or until golden brown. **Yield: 20 servings.**

Approx Per Serving: Cal 169; Prot 3 g; Carbo 19 g; Fiber 1 g;
    T Fat 9 g; 49% Calories from Fat; Chol 20 mg; Sod 352 mg.

Wenham Tea House

My Favorite Coffee Cake

³/₄ cup margarine, softened
1¹/₂ cups sugar
4 eggs, beaten
1 teaspoon vanilla extract
3 cups flour
1¹/₂ teaspoons baking soda

1¹/₂ teaspoons baking powder
2 cups sour cream
¹/₃ cup sugar
1 teaspoon cinnamon
¹/₄ cup finely chopped pecans

Cream margarine and 1¹/₂ cups sugar in bowl until light and fluffy. Add eggs and vanilla, beating well. Combine flour, baking soda and baking powder in small bowl. Add to creamed mixture alternately with sour cream, stirring well after each addition. Pour half the batter into 8-inch tube pan. Combine ¹/₃ cup sugar, cinnamon and pecans in small bowl. Sprinkle half the mixture over batter. Top with remaining batter and remaining cinnamon mixture. Bake at 350 degrees for 50 to 60 minutes or until golden brown. Cool for 30 minutes before serving.
Yield: 16 servings.

Approx Per Serving: Cal 344; Prot 5 g; Carbo 43 g; Fiber 1 g;
    T Fat 17 g; 45% Calories from Fat; Chol 66 mg; Sod 242 mg.

Ann O'Shea, WVIS Member

*For a brunch treat, butter toasted English
muffins, drizzle with honey and sprinkle with
almonds. Broil until heated through.*

Rohmflade

1 package frozen puff pastry,
  thawed
1 cup flour
1½ teaspoons ground aniseed

½ teaspoon salt
Pepper to taste
1 cup heavy cream

Unfold pastry onto lightly floured surface; roll out to 10-inch square. Place on ungreased baking sheet. Combine flour, aniseed, salt and pepper in medium bowl; mix well. Stir in heavy cream with fork until smooth. Spread over puff pastry to ½ inch from edges. Bake at 350 degrees for 30 to 40 minutes or until puffed and brown. Serve warm drizzled with honey. **Yield: 8 servings.**

Approx Per Serving: Cal 424; Prot 6 g; Carbo 35 g; Fiber <1 g;
  T Fat 28 g; 61% Calories from Fat; Chol 41 mg; Sod 438 mg.

Virginia L. Widmer, WVIS Member and Volunteer

Anadama Bread

1 package dry yeast
½ cup warm water
¼ teaspoon sugar
3 cups unbleached flour
½ cup stone-ground yellow
  cornmeal

1 teaspoon salt
½ cup canned cream-style corn
¼ cup molasses
2 tablespoons melted unsalted
  butter

Combine yeast, warm water and sugar in small bowl; let stand for 5 to 10 minutes. Combine flour, cornmeal and salt in large bowl; mix well. Combine corn, molasses and melted butter in medium bowl; mix well. Pour corn mixture and yeast mixture into flour mixture, stirring to form stiff dough. Knead on lightly floured surface for 10 minutes or until dough is smooth and elastic. Place in greased bowl, turning to coat surface. Let rise, covered, in warm place for 1 hour or until doubled in bulk. Punch dough down; flatten into 1-inch thick circle. Shape into loaf. Press into greased 5x9-inch loaf pan. Let rise, covered, for 1 hour or until doubled in bulk. Bake at 375 degrees for 35 minutes or until loaf tests done. Remove to wire rack to cool. **Yield: 12 servings.**

Approx Per Serving: Cal 162; Prot 4 g; Carbo 31 g; Fiber 1 g;
  T Fat 3 g; 14% Calories from Fat; Chol 5 mg; Sod 226 mg.

Wenham Tea House

Banana and All-Bran Bread

1/4 cup shortening
1/2 cup sugar
1 egg, beaten
1 cup All-Bran
1 1/2 cups mashed bananas
2 tablespoons water

1 teaspoon vanilla extract
1 1/2 cups flour
2 teaspoons baking powder
1/4 teaspoon salt
1/2 teaspoon baking soda

Cream shortening and sugar in mixer bowl until light and fluffy. Beat in egg. Stir in cereal, bananas, water and vanilla. Combine flour, baking powder, salt and baking soda in small bowl. Add to creamed mixture, stirring well. Pour into greased 5x9-inch loaf pan. Bake at 350 degrees for 1 hour or until loaf tests done. **Yield: 12 servings.**

Approx Per Serving: Cal 178; Prot 3 g; Carbo 32 g; Fiber 3 g;
    T Fat 5 g; 25% Calories from Fat; Chol 18 mg; Sod 221 mg.

Sally Taylor, Tea House Manager

Prize-Winning Banana Bread

2 cups flour
1 teaspoon baking powder
1 teaspoon salt
1/2 teaspoon baking soda
1 cup sugar

1/2 cup shortening
2 eggs, beaten
1 cup mashed bananas
1/2 cup chopped pecans

Sift together flour, baking powder, salt and baking soda in bowl. Cream sugar and shortening in mixer bowl until light and fluffy. Add eggs and bananas; mix well. Stir in dry ingredients and pecans. Pour into greased 5x9-inch loaf pan. Bake at 350 degrees for 60 to 70 minutes or until loaf tests done. **Yield: 12 servings.**

Approx Per Serving: Cal 279; Prot 4 g; Carbo 38 g; Fiber 1 g;
    T Fat 13 g; 41% Calories from Fat; Chol 36 mg; Sod 252 mg.

Ruth Stickney, Exchange Office Staff

*Easy Beer Bread is made with 3 cups self-rising
flour, 5 tablespoons sugar and one 12-ounce can beer.
Bake in a loaf pan at 350 degrees for 1 hour.*

Seven-Mound Cheese Puff Bread

1 cup milk
1/4 cup butter
1/8 teaspoon pepper

1 cup flour
4 eggs
1/2 cup shredded Swiss cheese

Combine milk, butter and pepper in saucepan. Bring to a boil. Add flour gradually, stirring until mixture pulls away from side of pan; remove from heat. Beat in eggs 1 at a time. Add half the cheese; mix well. Drop 7 spoonfuls of dough onto baking sheet to form circle. Drop 7 more spoonfuls on top of first layer, continuing until all dough is used. Sprinkle with remaining cheese. Bake at 375 degrees for 1 hour or until golden brown. Pull apart to serve. **Yield: 10 servings.**

Approx Per Serving: Cal 154; Prot 6 g; Carbo 11 g; Fiber <1 g;
T Fat 9 g; 55% Calories from Fat; Chol 106 mg; Sod 92 mg.

Barbara Younger, WVIS Member

Cinnamon Swirl Loaves

1 envelope dry yeast
1/4 cup warm water
2 cups milk, scalded
1/2 cup sugar
1/2 cup shortening
2 teaspoons salt

7 1/2 to 8 cups sifted flour
2 eggs, slightly beaten
3/4 cup sugar
1 1/2 tablespoons cinnamon
2 teaspoons water
1 tablespoon butter, softened

Dissolve yeast in warm water. Combine scalded milk, 1/2 cup sugar, shortening and salt in large bowl; cool. Add 3 cups flour; mix well. Stir in yeast and eggs; beat well. Add enough remaining flour to make soft dough. Knead on lightly floured surface for 8 to 10 minutes or until smooth and elastic. Place in greased bowl, turning to coat surface. Let rise, covered, in warm place for 1 to 2 hours or until doubled in bulk. Punch dough down; divide into 2 equal portions. Let stand, covered, for 10 minutes. Roll out to 7x15-inch rectangles. Combine 3/4 cup sugar and cinnamon in bowl; reserve 2 tablespoons of mixture. Sprinkle remaining mixture and 2 teaspoons water over rectangles; smooth with spatula. Roll up as for jelly roll, sealing seams. Place seam side down in greased 5x9-inch loaf pans. Let rise for 45 to 60 minutes or until almost doubled. Brush with softened butter; sprinkle with reserved cinnamon mixture. Bake at 375 degrees for 35 to 40 minutes or until loaves test done. **Yield: 24 servings.**

Approx Per Serving: Cal 243; Prot 5 g; Carbo 41 g; Fiber 1 g;
T Fat 6 g; 23% Calories from Fat; Chol 22 mg; Sod 197 mg.

Wenham Tea House

Nana O'Brien's Irish Bread

4 cups flour
1 cup sugar
4 teaspoons baking powder
2 teaspoons caraway seed
1/2 15-ounce package raisins

2 teaspoons margarine, softened
2 teaspoons salt
2 cups milk
2 eggs

Combine flour, sugar, baking powder, caraway seed, raisins, margarine and salt in large bowl; mix well. Knead until dough is smooth. Beat milk and eggs in small bowl. Pour into flour mixture gradually, stirring constantly until mixed. Pour into greased and floured 10-inch cast-iron skillet. Bake at 350 degrees for 1 1/4 hours. Cool in pan; cut into wedges. Serve with butter and sprinkle of sugar. **Yield: 16 servings.**

Approx Per Serving: Cal 286; Prot 5 g; Carbo 47 g; Fiber 1 g;
T Fat 2 g; 10% Calories from Fat; Chol 31 mg; Sod 352 mg.

Maureen Maestranzi, WVIS Member

Oatmeal Bread

1 1/2 cups boiling water
1 cup oats
3/4 cup molasses
3 tablespoons butter, softened

2 teaspoons salt
1 tablespoon yeast
2 cups warm water
8 cups flour

Pour boiling water over oats in bowl; let stand for 30 minutes. Add molasses, butter and salt; mix well. Dissolve yeast in warm water; add to oat mixture. Stir in enough flour to make soft dough. Knead on lightly floured surface for 10 minutes. Place in greased bowl, turning to coat surface. Let rise, covered, until doubled in bulk. Punch dough down; knead again. Shape into loaves; place in greased loaf pans. Bake at 400 degrees for 5 minutes. Reduce temperature to 350 degrees. Bake for 30 to 40 minutes longer. Serve with melted butter. **Yield: 48 servings.**

Approx Per Serving: Cal 100; Prot 3 g; Carbo 20 g; Fiber 1 g;
T Fat 1 g; 9% Calories from Fat; Chol 2 mg; Sod 96 mg.

Wenham Tea House

Whip applesauce with light margarine to make
a low-calorie spread for breads.

Yummy Sweet Rolls

1 cup sour cream, scalded
1/2 cup melted butter
1/2 cup sugar
1 teaspoon salt
2 envelopes dry yeast
1/2 cup warm water
2 eggs, beaten
4 cups flour
3/4 cup sugar

16 ounces cream cheese, softened
1 egg
2 teaspoons vanilla extract
1/2 teaspoon salt
2 cups confectioners' sugar, sifted
1/4 cup milk
2 teaspoons vanilla extract

Combine first 4 ingredients in bowl; mix well. Dissolve yeast in warm water in large bowl. Stir in sour cream mixture and 2 eggs. Add flour, stirring to form soft dough. Chill, covered, overnight. Divide dough into 4 equal portions. Knead each portion on lightly floured surface 4 to 5 times. Roll to 8x12-inch rectangles. Beat 3/4 cup sugar, cream cheese, 1 egg, 2 teaspoons vanilla and 1/2 teaspoon salt in mixer bowl until light and fluffy. Spread over dough to 1/2 inch of edges. Roll as for jelly roll, sealing edges. Cut into 1 1/2-inch slices. Place cut sides down 2 inches apart on baking sheets. Let rise, covered, in warm place for 1 1/2 hours or until doubled in bulk. Bake at 375 degrees for 12 minutes or until golden brown. Drizzle with mixture of confectioners' sugar, milk and 2 teaspoons vanilla. **Yield: 30 servings.**

Approx Per Serving: Cal 230; Prot 4 g; Carbo 30 g; Fiber 1 g;
    T Fat 11 g; 42% Calories from Fat; Chol 50 mg; Sod 190 mg.

Wenham Tea House

Best Blueberry Muffins

6 tablespoons butter, softened
1 1/4 cups sugar
2 eggs
2 cups flour
1/2 teaspoon salt

2 teaspoons baking powder
1/2 cup milk
1 pint fresh blueberries
2 teaspoons sugar
1/8 teaspoon cinnamon

Grease muffin cups; line with paper baking cups. Cream butter and 1 1/4 cups sugar in mixer bowl until light and fluffy. Beat in eggs 1 at a time. Sift flour, salt and baking powder together. Add to creamed mixture alternately with milk. Crush 1/2 cup blueberries with fork; stir into batter. Fold in remaining blueberries. Fill muffin cups 7/8 full. Sprinkle with mixture of 2 teaspoons sugar and cinnamon. Bake at 375 degrees for 30 minutes or until brown. Cool in pan for 30 minutes; remove to wire rack to cool completely. **Yield: 16 servings.**

Approx Per Serving: Cal 183; Prot 3 g; Carbo 31 g; Fiber 1 g;
    T Fat 5 g; 27% Calories from Fat; Chol 39 mg; Sod 158 mg.

Wenham Tea House

Endless Bran Muffins

2 cups boiling water
2 cups All-Bran
1   15-ounce package raisins
1 cup sugar
1 cup corn oil
2 cups molasses

4 eggs, beaten
1 quart buttermilk
3 cups bran flakes
7 cups flour
7 teaspoons baking soda
1 teaspoon salt

Pour boiling water over 2 cups All-Bran and raisins in bowl; set aside. Combine sugar, oil, molasses, eggs, buttermilk and bran flakes in large bowl; mix well. Stir in cooled raisin mixture. Add flour, baking soda and salt; mix thoroughly. Spoon into greased muffin cups, filling 2/3 full. Bake at 400 degrees for 20 minutes. May store batter in refrigerator for up to 2 months. Note: To avoid risk of salmonella, use no-cholesterol egg substitute for eggs or prepare batter, bake all muffins and reheat muffins in microwave as desired. **Yield: 72 servings.**

Approx Per Serving: Cal 141; Prot 3 g; Carbo 26 g; Fiber 2 g;
    T Fat 4 g; 23% Calories from Fat; Chol 12 mg; Sod 175 mg.

Wenham Tea House

Refrigerator Bran Muffins

2½ cups sifted flour
2½ teaspoons baking soda
1 teaspoon salt
1 cup boiling water
1 cup All-Bran

1 cup sugar
½ cup shortening
2 eggs, well beaten
2 cups buttermilk
2 cups bran buds

Sift flour, baking soda and salt together; set aside. Pour boiling water over cereal in bowl; set aside. Cream sugar and shortening in large bowl until light and fluffy. Add eggs, beating well. Stir in buttermilk, bran buds and cereal mixture. Add sifted dry ingredients, mixing thoroughly. Spoon into greased muffin cups, filling 3/4 full. Bake at 400 degrees for 20 minutes. May add raisins. May store mixture in refrigerator for up to 6 weeks. Note: To avoid risk of salmonella, use no-cholesterol egg substitute for eggs or prepare batter, bake all muffins and reheat muffins in microwave as desired. **Yield: 30 servings.**

Approx Per Serving: Cal 124; Prot 3 g; Carbo 21 g; Fiber 3 g;
    T Fat 4 g; 28% Calories from Fat; Chol 15 mg; Sod 228 mg.

Wenham Tea House

Carrot Muffins

1½ cups flour
1 cup sugar
1 teaspoon each baking powder,
   baking soda and cinnamon
½ teaspoon salt

⅔ cup oil
2 eggs, beaten
¾ cup finely grated carrots
½ cup drained crushed pineapple
1 teaspoon vanilla extract

Sift dry ingredients into bowl. Add oil; stir until moistened. Beat in eggs. Add carrots, pineapple and vanilla. Beat for 2 minutes. Spoon into greased muffin cups. Bake at 325 degrees for 25 minutes. **Yield: 20 servings.**

Approx Per Serving: Cal 149; Prot 2 g; Carbo 19 g; Fiber <1 g;
   T Fat 8 g; 47% Calories from Fat; Chol 21 mg; Sod 120 mg.

Wenham Tea House

Cranberry-Orange Muffins

3½ cups flour
¼ cup sugar
4 teaspoons baking powder
1 teaspoon salt
2 eggs, beaten

½ cup orange juice
⅔ cup oil
2 cups fresh cranberries
¼ cup sugar

Combine first 4 ingredients in large bowl. Make well in center. Beat eggs with orange juice and oil. Pour into well; stir until moistened. Toss cranberries with ¼ cup sugar. Fold into batter. Fill greased muffin cups ⅔ full. Sprinkle with additional sugar if desired. Bake at 400 degrees for 18 to 20 minutes or until brown. **Yield: 30 servings.**

Approx Per Serving: Cal 119; Prot 2 g; Carbo 16 g; Fiber 1 g;
   T Fat 5 g; 40% Calories from Fat; Chol 14 mg; Sod 120 mg.

Wenham Tea House

Twin Mountain Muffins

8 cups flour
¼ cup baking powder
2 teaspoons salt
½ cup sugar

8 eggs, beaten
4 cups milk
1 cup melted butter

Combine dry ingredients in large bowl. Beat eggs with milk and melted butter in bowl. Stir into dry ingredients. Fill greased muffin cups ⅔ full. Bake at 400 degrees for 15 minutes. **Yield: 48 servings.**

Approx Per Serving: Cal 145; Prot 4 g; Carbo 19 g; Fiber 1 g;
   T Fat 6 g; 35% Calories from Fat; Chol 49 mg; Sod 224 mg.

Wenham Tea House

Morning Glory Muffins

4 cups flour
2½ cups sugar
4 teaspoons baking soda
4 teaspoons cinnamon
1 teaspoon salt
4 cups grated carrots
1 cup raisins

1 cup chopped pecans
1 cup shredded coconut
2 apples, peeled, grated
6 eggs
2 cups oil
4 teaspoons vanilla extract

Combine flour, sugar, baking soda, cinnamon and salt in large bowl; mix well. Stir in carrots, raisins, pecans, coconut and apples. Beat eggs with oil in small bowl. Add to dry ingredients with vanilla, stirring until moistened. Spoon into buttered muffin cups, filling to top. Bake at 350 degrees for 35 minutes. Cool on wire rack for 5 minutes. **Yield: 30 servings.**

Approx Per Serving: Cal 341; Prot 4 g; Carbo 39 g; Fiber 2 g;
    T Fat 20 g; 51% Calories from Fat; Chol 43 mg; Sod 209 mg.

Wenham Tea House

Texas Muffins

3 cups whole wheat flour
2 cups unbleached flour
4 teaspoons baking soda
1½ teaspoons salt
2 teaspoons cinnamon
½ teaspoon ground ginger
½ teaspoon nutmeg
½ teaspoon ground cloves

½ teaspoon mace
1 cup unsalted butter, softened
2 teaspoons vanilla extract
2½ cups packed brown sugar
4 eggs, beaten
3 cups applesauce
2 cups raisins
3 cups chopped walnuts

Sift wheat flour, unbleached flour, baking soda, salt, cinnamon, ginger, nutmeg, cloves and mace together. Cream butter with vanilla and brown sugar in mixer bowl until light and fluffy. Beat in eggs. Add dry ingredients alternately with applesauce, beating at low speed until mixed. Stir in raisins and walnuts. Spoon into greased muffin cups. Bake at 350 degrees for 25 minutes or until brown. **Yield: 30 servings.**

Approx Per Serving: Cal 346; Prot 5 g; Carbo 52 g; Fiber 3 g;
    T Fat 15 g; 37% Calories from Fat; Chol 45 mg; Sod 291 mg.

Wenham Tea House

Wenham Museum

Desserts

Apple Crisp

2 cups flour
1 cup packed brown sugar
1/2 teaspoon salt
3/4 cup oats
1/2 cup butter, softened

7 to 8 apples, sliced
1 cup sugar
3/4 cup butter
2 tablespoons cornstarch
1 cup boiling water

Combine flour, brown sugar, salt and oats in bowl. Cut in 1/2 cup butter until mixture is crumbly. Spread half the mixture into 9x13-inch baking pan. Arrange sliced apples over top. Combine sugar, 3/4 cup butter, cornstarch and boiling water in saucepan. Bring to a boil. Cook until thickened, stirring constantly. Pour over apples. Top with remaining crumb mixture. Bake at 375 degrees for 40 minutes. **Yield: 15 servings.**

Approx Per Serving: Cal 374; Prot 3 g; Carbo 57 g; Fiber 2 g;
     T Fat 16 g; 37% Calories from Fat; Chol 41 mg; Sod 209 mg.

Wenham Tea House

Apple Crumble

4 cups sliced peeled apples
1/2 to 3/4 cup packed light
   brown sugar
1/8 teaspoon cinnamon
1/4 cup water

1 cup flour
1/2 cup packed dark brown
   sugar
1/3 cup butter, softened

Arrange apple slices in buttered baking dish. Sprinkle with light brown sugar, cinnamon and water. Combine flour and dark brown sugar in bowl. Cut in butter until mixture is crumbly. Spread evenly over apples. Bake at 350 degrees for 50 minutes or until brown and bubbly. **Yield: 15 servings.**

Approx Per Serving: Cal 169; Prot 1 g; Carbo 33 g; Fiber 1 g;
     T Fat 4 g; 22% Calories from Fat; Chol 11 mg; Sod 45 mg.

Wenham Tea House

*For **Apricot Mousse**, combine 1 cup apricot pulp, 3 egg whites, 1/4 cup sugar, 2 tablespoons lemon juice, 3 drops of almond extract and the grated rind of 1 orange. Beat until stiff peaks form and chill until serving time.*

Cheesy Dapper Apple Squares

1½ cups flour
1½ cups graham cracker
  crumbs
1 cup packed brown sugar
½ teaspoon baking soda

¾ cup butter, softened
6 slices American cheese
2½ cups sliced peeled apples
¾ cup sugar
½ cup chopped pecans

Combine flour, graham cracker crumbs, brown sugar and baking soda in bowl. Cut in butter until crumbly. Reserve 1½ cups crumbs. Press remaining crumbs into 9x13-inch baking pan. Layer cheese slices and apples into prepared pan. Sprinkle with sugar, reserved crumb mixture and pecans. Bake at 350 degrees for 35 to 40 minutes or until golden brown. Serve warm. **Yield: 15 servings.**

Approx Per Serving: Cal 365; Prot 5 g; Carbo 50 g; Fiber 1 g;
  T Fat 17 g; 41% Calories from Fat; Chol 36 mg; Sod 349 mg.

Wenham Tea House

Apple-Cranberry Crisp

5 cups chopped apples
8 ounces whole cranberries
1½ cups sugar
½ cup butter, melted

1 cup oats
½ cup flour
½ cup packed brown sugar
½ cup chopped pecans

Toss apples and cranberries with sugar in bowl. Arrange in greased baking dish. Combine melted butter with oats, flour, brown sugar and pecans in bowl; mix well. Sprinkle over fruit. Bake at 350 degrees for 1 hour. **Yield: 15 servings.**

Approx Per Serving: Cal 259; Prot 2 g; Carbo 45 g; Fiber 3 g;
  T Fat 9 g; 31% Calories from Fat; Chol 17 mg; Sod 57 mg.

Wenham Tea House

*Make **Apple Brown Betty** by creaming ½ cup sugar and ¼ cup shortening. Beat in ⅓ cup molasses and ½ teaspoon cinnamon. Stir in cubes of 6 slices of bread and 4 chopped apples. Bake, covered, at 375 degrees for 30 minutes and uncovered for 45 minutes longer.*

Danish Apple Dessert

1/2 cup melted margarine
1 6-ounce package Zwieback, crushed
1 teaspoon almond extract

1 15-ounce jar applesauce
1/2 cup whipping cream
1 teaspoon vanilla extract
1 tablespoon sugar

Combine melted margarine, crushed Zwieback and almond extract in bowl; mix well. Alternate layers of 1/3 of the crumbs and half the applesauce in 9-inch round dish, pressing down with spatula. Chill in refrigerator until firm. Beat whipping cream with vanilla and sugar in mixer bowl until soft peaks form. Spread over top layer. Garnish with chopped nuts and cherries. **Yield: 8 servings.**

Approx Per Serving: Cal 293; Prot 3 g; Carbo 29 g; Fiber 1 g;
    T Fat 19 g; 57% Calories from Fat; Chol 20 mg; Sod 196 mg.

Wenham Tea House

Apple Pan Dowdy

3 cups sliced tart apples
1/2 teaspoon nutmeg
1/2 teaspoon cinnamon
1/4 teaspoon salt
1/2 cup packed brown sugar
1 1/2 cups flour

2 teaspoons baking powder
1/2 cup sugar
1/2 teaspoon salt
1/2 cup butter
1/2 cup milk
1 egg, beaten

Arrange apples in baking pan. Sprinkle with mixture of nutmeg, cinnamon, 1/4 teaspoon salt and brown sugar. Bake, covered with foil, at 350 degrees for 30 minutes. Combine flour, baking powder, sugar and 1/2 teaspoon salt in bowl; mix well. Melt butter in saucepan; remove from heat. Beat in milk and egg. Add to flour mixture, stirring until moistened. Pour over apples. Bake for 30 minutes or until golden brown. **Yield: 15 servings.**

Approx Per Serving: Cal 183; Prot 2 g; Carbo 29 g; Fiber 1 g;
    T Fat 7 g; 34% Calories from Fat; Chol 32 mg; Sod 215 mg.

Wenham Tea House

*Create a quick dessert with fresh fruit slices,
a dollop of sour cream or yogurt and a sprinkle
of brown sugar or coconut.*

Blueberry-Apple Crisp

2 cups blueberries
2 cups sliced peeled tart apples
1 tablespoon lemon juice
1/2 cup packed light brown
   sugar
1 cup flour

3/4 cup sugar
1 teaspoon baking powder
3/4 teaspoon salt
1 egg, slightly beaten
1/3 cup melted butter
1/2 teaspoon cinnamon

Layer blueberries and apples in shallow buttered 1 1/2-quart baking dish. Sprinkle with lemon juice and brown sugar. Combine flour, sugar, baking powder and salt in bowl; mix well. Add egg, stirring until crumbly. Sprinkle over fruit; drizzle with melted butter. Dust with cinnamon. Bake at 350 degrees for 35 to 40 minutes or until golden brown. Serve warm with cream. **Yield: 6 servings.**

Approx Per Serving: Cal 411; Prot 4 g; Carbo 76 g; Fiber 3 g;
   T Fat 12 g; 25% Calories from Fat; Chol 63 mg; Sod 432 mg.

Wenham Tea House

Blueberry-Cream Cheese Squares

1/4 cup cornstarch
1/2 cup sugar
1/2 cup water
3 cups blueberries
1 13-ounce package graham
   cracker crumbs

1/4 cup melted butter
16 ounces cream cheese,
   softened
1/2 cup sugar
2 teaspoons vanilla extract
9 ounces whipped topping

Combine cornstarch, 1/2 cup sugar, water and blueberries in saucepan. Cook over medium heat until thickened and bubbly, stirring constantly; cool. Combine graham cracker crumbs and 1/4 cup melted butter in bowl. Press half the crumb mixture into foil-lined 9x13-inch pan. Beat cream cheese with 1/2 cup sugar and vanilla in mixer bowl until light and fluffy. Fold in whipped topping. Spread half the cream cheese mixture gently over crumb mixture. Layer with blueberries, remaining cream cheese mixture and remaining crumb mixture. Chill in refrigerator overnight. Transfer to serving plate; cut into squares to serve. **Yield: 15 servings.**

Approx Per Serving: Cal 369; Prot 5 g; Carbo 43 g; Fiber 1 g;
   T Fat 21 g; 49% Calories from Fat; Chol 41 mg; Sod 273 mg.

Wenham Tea House

New England Blueberry Slump

1 cup blueberries
2 teaspoons cinnamon
1 tablespoon grated lemon rind
2/3 cup packed brown sugar
1/3 cup shortening
3/4 cup sugar
1 teaspoon salt
1 egg, beaten

1¼ cups flour
2 teaspoons baking powder
1½ cups milk
1 teaspoon vanilla extract
1 cup blueberries
1/2 cup sugar
Juice of 1 lemon
1/2 cup rum

Combine 1 cup blueberries, cinnamon, lemon rind and brown sugar in bowl; mix well. Spoon into buttered 9-inch round baking dish. Cream shortening, 3/4 cup sugar and salt in mixer bowl until light and fluffy. Stir in egg. Mix flour and baking powder together. Mix milk and vanilla in small bowl. Stir into creamed mixture alternately with flour mixture. Spoon over blueberries. Bake at 350 degrees for 40 to 45 minutes or until bubbly. Invert onto serving plate. Combine remaining 1 cup blueberries, 1/2 cup sugar, lemon juice and rum in saucepan. Cook over medium heat until sugar is dissolved, stirring constantly. Serve warm over blueberry dessert. May top with ice cream. **Yield: 6 servings.**

Approx Per Serving: Cal 594; Prot 6 g; Carbo 102 g; Fiber 2 g;
    T Fat 15 g; 23% Calories from Fat; Chol 44 mg; Sod 520 mg.

Wenham Tea House

Cranberry Trenton Dessert

3 cups chopped cranberries
3 cups chopped apples
1 tablespoon cornstarch
1/3 cup packed brown sugar
3/4 cup sugar
1/2 teaspoon salt
1 teaspoon vanilla extract
1 cup instant oats

1/2 cup packed brown sugar
1/3 cup flour
2 tablespoons crushed
  cornflakes
1/2 teaspoon salt
1/4 cup butter
1/2 cup chopped pecans

Combine cranberries, apples, cornstarch, 1/3 cup brown sugar, sugar, salt and vanilla in bowl; mix well. Pour into baking pan. Combine oats, 1/2 cup brown sugar, flour, cornflakes and 1/2 teaspoon salt in bowl. Cut in butter until mixture is crumbly. Stir in pecans. Sprinkle over cranberry mixture. Bake at 350 degrees for 35 to 40 minutes or until golden brown. **Yield: 10 servings.**

Approx Per Serving: Cal 297; Prot 2 g; Carbo 57 g; Fiber 3 g;
    T Fat 8 g; 23% Calories from Fat; Chol 12 mg; Sod 273 mg.

Wenham Tea House

Pumpkin Squares

4 eggs, beaten
1²/₃ cups sugar
1 cup oil
1 16-ounce can pumpkin
2 cups flour

2 teaspoons baking powder
2 teaspoons cinnamon
1 teaspoon baking soda
¹/₈ teaspoon salt
Cream Cheese Frosting

Beat eggs, sugar, oil and pumpkin together in large bowl. Combine flour, baking powder, cinnamon, baking soda and salt in bowl; mix well. Stir into pumpkin mixture. Pour into 9x13-inch baking pan. Bake at 350 degrees for 25 to 30 minutes or until golden brown. Cool in pan for several minutes. Spread Cream Cheese Frosting over cooled pumpkin layer. Cut into squares to serve. May substitute canned squash for pumpkin. **Yield: 36 servings.**

Cream Cheese Frosting

¹/₂ cup margarine, softened
3 ounces cream cheese, softened

1³/₄ cups confectioners' sugar
1 teaspoon vanilla extract

Cream margarine, cream cheese, confectioners' sugar and vanilla in mixer bowl until light and fluffy.

Approx Per Serving: Cal 181; Prot 2 g; Carbo 22 g; Fiber <1 g;
    T Fat 10 g; 50% Calories from Fat; Chol 26 mg; Sod 94 mg.

Wenham Tea House

Rhubarb Crunch

1 cup flour
³/₄ cup rolled oats
1 cup packed brown sugar
1 teaspoon cinnamon
¹/₂ cup melted butter

4 cups chopped rhubarb
1 cup sugar
2 tablespoons cornstarch
1 cup water
1 teaspoon vanilla extract

Combine flour, oats, brown sugar and cinnamon in bowl. Stir in butter until crumbly. Press half the crumb mixture into 9x9-inch baking pan. Cover with chopped rhubarb. Mix sugar, cornstarch, water and vanilla in saucepan. Cook over medium heat for 10 minutes or until thickened, stirring constantly. Pour over rhubarb. Top with remaining crumb mixture. Bake at 350 degrees for 1 hour. Cut into squares to serve. Garnish with ice cream or whipped cream. **Yield: 15 servings.**

Approx Per Serving: Cal 231; Prot 2 g; Carbo 42 g; Fiber 2 g;
    T Fat 7 g; 25% Calories from Fat; Chol 17 mg; Sod 62 mg.

Wenham Tea House

International Delight

3 egg whites
1/2 teaspoon baking powder
1 cup sugar
1 cup chopped pecans
40 butter crackers, crushed
8 ounces cream cheese, softened

9 ounces whipped topping
1 16-ounce can pineapple,
   drained
1 16-ounce can fruit cocktail,
   drained

Beat egg whites with baking powder in mixer bowl until foamy. Add sugar gradually, beating until stiff peaks form. Fold in pecans and crushed crackers. Press into greased 9x13-inch baking pan. Bake at 350 degrees for 20 minutes; cool. Beat cream cheese and whipped topping in bowl until light and fluffy. Fold in pineapple and fruit cocktail. Spread over prepared crust. Chill in refrigerator until firm. Cut into squares to serve. **Yield: 15 servings.**

Approx Per Serving: Cal 288; Prot 3 g; Carbo 33 g; Fiber 1 g;
    T Fat 18 g; 52% Calories from Fat; Chol 17 mg; Sod 153 mg.

Wenham Tea House

New York-Style Cherry-Cheese Squares

1½ cups graham cracker
   crumbs
16 ounces cream cheese,
   softened
3/4 cup sugar
1 tablespoon vanilla extract
2 eggs, beaten

1/8 teaspoon cinnamon
2 cups sour cream
2 tablespoons sugar
1 teaspoon vanilla extract
1 21-ounce can cherry pie
   filling

Line 9-inch square baking pan with graham cracker crumbs. Beat cream cheese, 3/4 cup sugar, 1 tablespoon vanilla, eggs and cinnamon at low speed in mixer bowl until smooth. Spread into prepared pan. Bake at 375 degrees for 20 minutes. Turn off oven. Let stand in oven for 5 minutes with door open. Remove and cool for 20 minutes. Combine sour cream, 2 tablespoons sugar and 1 teaspoon vanilla in small bowl; mix well. Pour over cooled cheese mixture. Bake at 450 degrees for 5 minutes; cool. Drain pie filling, reserving both cherries and sauce. Spoon cherry sauce over sour cream layer. Cut into small squares; place in paper baking cups. Garnish with cherries. **Yield: 20 servings.**

Approx Per Serving: Cal 208; Prot 4 g; Carbo 17 g; Fiber <1 g;
    T Fat 14 g; 60% Calories from Fat; Chol 56 mg; Sod 142 mg.
    Nutritional information does not include pie filling.

Wenham Tea House

Brazilian Coffee Cream Puffs

1 cup butter
1/8 teaspoon salt
2 cups boiling water
2 cups flour
8 eggs

1/4 cup cold strong coffee
1 teaspoon sugar
2 cups heavy cream, whipped
Rum Sauce

Combine butter, salt and water in saucepan. Cook over high heat until butter melts, stirring occasionally. Remove from heat. Add flour; beat until mixture forms smooth ball. Beat in eggs 1 at a time. Shape into 1-inch balls. Place on greased baking sheet. Bake at 400 degrees for 10 minutes. Reduce temperature to 350 degrees. Bake for 15 minutes or until light brown. Cool; cut into halves. Fold coffee and sugar into whipped cream. Spoon into puffs; place on plates. Serve with Rum Sauce. **Yield: 30 servings.**

Rum Sauce

2 egg yolks, beaten
1 cup sifted confectioners' sugar
6 tablespoons rum

1 teaspoon vanilla extract
1 cup whipping cream, whipped

Beat egg yolks with confectioners' sugar until dissolved. Beat in rum gradually. Fold vanilla into whipped cream. Fold in egg mixture.

Approx Per Serving: Cal 212; Prot 3 g; Carbo 11 g; Fiber <1 g;
    T Fat 17 g; 72% Calories from Fat; Chol 120 mg; Sod 89 mg.

Wenham Tea House

Custard Angel Squares

1 envelope unflavored gelatin
1/4 cup milk
3/4 cup sugar
1/2 teaspoon salt
13/4 cups milk
4 egg yolks, beaten

2 teaspoons vanilla extract
4 egg whites
1/4 cup sugar
1 cup whipping cream, whipped
1 prepared angel food cake,
    cubed

Soften gelatin in 1/4 cup milk in small bowl. Mix with next 4 ingredients in double boiler. Cook over simmering water until thickened, stirring constantly. Stir in vanilla. Chill until partially set. Beat egg whites in mixer bowl until foamy. Add remaining 1/4 cup sugar, beating until soft peaks form. Fold egg whites and whipped cream into custard. Line 9x13-inch pan with cake. Pour custard over top. Chill for 4 hours to overnight. Cut into squares. Serve with strawberries. **Yield: 15 servings.**

Approx Per Serving: Cal 249; Prot 6 g; Carbo 38 g; Fiber <1 g;
    T Fat 9 g; 30% Calories from Fat; Chol 83 mg; Sod 322 mg.

Wenham Tea House

Cream Puffs

1 cup sugar
3 tablespoons flour
3 tablespoons cornstarch
3/4 teaspoon salt
4 1/2 cups milk
3 egg yolks, beaten
1 tablespoon vanilla extract
1 1/2 cups whipping cream,
  whipped
1/2 cup butter

1 cup boiling water
1 cup flour
1/4 teaspoon salt
4 eggs
1/3 cup butter
2 cups confectioners' sugar
2 ounces unsweetened
  chocolate, melted
1 1/2 teaspoons vanilla extract
2 to 4 tablespoons hot water

Combine sugar, flour, cornstarch and 3/4 teaspoon salt in saucepan. Stir in milk. Bring to a boil, stirring constantly. Cook for 2 to 3 minutes longer or until thickened, stirring constantly. Stir 1 tablespoon hot mixture into egg yolks; beat well. Stir eggs into custard mixture. Bring to a boil. Add vanilla, stirring well. Cool. Beat until smooth; fold in whipped cream. Combine butter and boiling water in saucepan, stirring until melted. Add flour and salt. Cook until mixture is smooth and forms soft ball, stirring vigorously. Cool slightly. Beat in eggs 1 at a time until smooth. Drop by teaspoonfuls onto greased baking sheet or force through pastry bag with 1/2 to 1-inch tips for eclairs. Bake at 400 degrees for 10 minutes. Reduce temperature to 350 degrees. Bake for 10 to 15 minutes longer or until light brown. Cool. Slice into halves. Fill with prepared custard; replace tops. Melt 1/3 cup butter in saucepan. Add 2 cups confectioners' sugar, chocolate and 1 1/2 teaspoons vanilla. Stir in water, 1 tablespoon at a time until glaze is of desired consistency. Drizzle over cream puffs. **Yield: 12 servings.**

Approx Per Serving: Cal 531; Prot 8 g; Carbo 54 g; Fiber 1 g;
    T Fat 33 g; 54% Calories from Fat; Chol 212 mg; Sod 360 mg.

Wenham Tea House

Lemon Ice Cream

4 cups half and half
2 cups sugar
2 tablespoons freshly grated
  lemon rind

2/3 cup freshly squeezed lemon
  juice

Combine half and half and sugar in bowl, stirring until dissolved. Stir in lemon rind and juice. Pour into 9x13-inch pan or individual dessert dishes. Freeze for several hours or until firm. **Yield: 12 servings.**

Approx Per Serving: Cal 237; Prot 2 g; Carbo 38 g; Fiber <1 g;
    T Fat 9 g; 34% Calories from Fat; Chol 30 mg; Sod 34 mg.

Barbara Ireland, WVIS Member

Lemon Meringues

2 egg whites
6 tablespoons sugar
1 teaspoon vanilla extract
2 tablespoons sugar
5 tablespoons cornstarch
1/2 teaspoon salt

1 cup sugar
1 1/2 cups boiling water
3 egg yolks, beaten
Juice and grated rind of 2
lemons

Beat egg whites in mixer bowl until stiff and dry. Add 6 tablespoons sugar, 1 tablespoon at a time beating constantly until stiff peaks form. Fold in vanilla and remaining 2 tablespoons sugar. Shape with tablespoon or pastry bag on baking sheet lined with parchment paper. Bake at 250 degrees for 50 minutes. Remove gently from baking sheet; cool on plate. Combine cornstarch, salt and sugar in saucepan. Add boiling water. Cook until thickened, stirring constantly. Beat egg yolks with lemon juice and rind. Add a small amount of cooked mixture to egg yolks; beat well. Add egg yolk mixture to cooked mixture, beating constantly. Cook until thickened, stirring constantly; cool. Spoon into baked meringues. **Yield: 8 servings.**

Approx Per Serving: Cal 194; Prot 2 g; Carbo 43 g; Fiber <1 g;
    T Fat 2 g; 10% Calories from Fat; Chol 80 mg; Sod 150 mg.

Wenham Tea House

Lemon Sauce and Fruit

2 egg yolks
1/3 cup sugar
1/3 cup melted margarine
1 tablespoon grated lemon rind
2 tablespoons fresh lemon juice
1/3 cup heavy cream, whipped

1   16-ounce can black Bing
    cherries, drained
1   20-ounce can chunk
    pineapple, drained
3 bananas, sliced

Beat egg yolks in mixer bowl until thickened. Add sugar, beating until lemon-colored. Add melted margarine, lemon rind and juice; mix well. Fold in whipped cream; chill. Combine cherries, pineapple and bananas in bowl. Spoon into individual serving dishes. Top with lemon sauce. **Yield: 6 servings.**

Approx Per Serving: Cal 343; Prot 3 g; Carbo 48 g; Fiber 3 g;
    T Fat 17 g; 43% Calories from Fat; Chol 89 mg; Sod 129 mg.

Suzanne McCarthy, Chairman, Special Projects, WVIS

Frosted Mint Delight

2 16-ounce cans crushed
  pineapple
¾ cup mint-flavored apple jelly
1 envelope unflavored gelatin

2 cups whipping cream
2 tablespoons confectioners'
  sugar

Drain pineapple, reserving 1 cup juice. Mix pineapple with jelly in saucepan. Cook over low heat until jelly is melted, stirring frequently. Soften gelatin in reserved pineapple juice. Stir into hot pineapple mixture until gelatin dissolves. Whip cream in mixer bowl until soft peaks form. Add confectioners' sugar; beat until stiff peaks form. Fold into pineapple mixture. Freeze until partially set. Spoon into parfait glasses. Garnish with additional whipped cream. **Yield: 12 servings.**

Approx Per Serving: Cal 263; Prot 2 g; Carbo 33 g; Fiber 1 g;
  T Fat 15 g; 49% Calories from Fat; Chol 54 mg; Sod 21 mg.

Wenham Tea House

Orange Cream

1 cup heavy cream
1 cup sour cream
½ cup sugar
1 envelope unflavored gelatin

Juice and grated rind of 1
  orange
3 tablespoons orange liqueur
1 cup sliced strawberries

Combine heavy cream, sour cream and sugar in saucepan. Heat gently, stirring frequently. Soften gelatin in orange juice in small bowl. Stir into cream mixture with orange rind. Cook until gelatin dissolves, stirring constantly. Stir in liqueur and strawberries. Pour into dessert goblets; chill. Garnish with additional strawberries. **Yield: 6 servings.**

Approx Per Serving: Cal 341; Prot 3 g; Carbo 28 g; Fiber 2 g;
  T Fat 23 g; 62% Calories from Fat; Chol 71 mg; Sod 38 mg.

Wenham Tea House

Piña Colada Wedges

8 ounces cream cheese, softened
1/3 cup sugar
2 tablespoons rum
2 cups whipped topping
2 cups flaked coconut

1 8-ounce can crushed
  pineapple in syrup
1½ cups whipped topping
2/3 cup flaked coconut

Beat cream cheese with sugar and rum in mixer bowl until light and fluffy. Fold in 2 cups whipped topping, 2 cups coconut and undrained pineapple. Spread in 8-inch round pan. Spread with remaining 1½ cups whipped topping; sprinkle with remaining 2/3 cup coconut. Freeze for 2 hours or until firm. Cut into wedges to serve. Garnish with additional pineapple and cherries. May substitute ½ teaspoon rum extract for rum. **Yield: 12 servings.**

Approx Per Serving: Cal 252; Prot 2 g; Carbo 22 g; Fiber 2 g;
    T Fat 18 g; 62% Calories from Fat; Chol 21 mg; Sod 65 mg.

Wenham Tea House

Prune Whip

3 envelopes unflavored gelatin
1/2 cup cold water
1/3 cup boiling water
1⅓ cups confectioners' sugar

2 teaspoons lemon juice
1⅓ cups prune purée
4 egg whites
1 tablespoon sugar

Soften gelatin in cold water in mixer bowl for 10 minutes. Add boiling water, stirring until gelatin is dissolved. Add confectioners' sugar, lemon juice and prune purée; mix well. Chill until partially set. Beat at high speed until light and fluffy. Beat egg whites in mixer bowl until foamy. Add 1 tablespoon sugar, beating constantly until stiff peaks form. Fold into prune mixture. Spoon into parfait glasses. Garnish with whipped cream or custard sauce. May substitute apricot juice for boiling water and apricot purée for prune purée. **Yield: 4 servings.**

Approx Per Serving: Cal 353; Prot 10 g; Carbo 83 g; Fiber 7 g;
    T Fat <1 g; 1% Calories from Fat; Chol 0 mg; Sod 58 mg.

Wenham Tea House

Chop raisins in a food processor or blender. To keep them from getting sticky, add 1 teaspoon of oil or a small amount of flour from ingredients called for in recipe.

Blueberry Pudding

2 cups blueberries
Juice of 1 lemon
1/2 teaspoon cinnamon
3 tablespoons butter, softened
1 3/4 cups sugar
1/2 cup milk

1 teaspoon baking powder
1/4 teaspoon salt
1 cup flour
1 tablespoon cornstarch
Salt to taste
1 cup boiling water

Mix first 3 ingredients in bowl. Spread in greased baking dish. Cream butter and 3/4 cup sugar in mixer bowl. Add milk and sifted baking powder, 1/4 teaspoon salt and flour; mix well. Spread over blueberries. Sprinkle with mixture of 1 cup sugar, cornstarch and salt. Pour boiling water over all; do not stir. Bake at 375 degrees for 1 hour. Serve warm. **Yield: 6 servings.**

Nutritional information for this recipe is not available.

Wenham Tea House

Stove-Top Chocolate Bread Pudding

1 ounce unsweetened chocolate
1 1/2 cups milk
2 cups cubed bread
1 egg, beaten

1/4 cup sugar
1/8 teaspoon salt
1 teaspoon vanilla extract
8 large marshmallows

Melt chocolate in milk in double boiler over boiling water, stirring frequently. Add bread, egg, sugar and salt. Cook for 5 minutes, stirring frequently. Fold in vanilla and marshmallows cut into fourths. Serve warm with cream. **Yield: 4 servings.**

Approx Per Serving: Cal 249; Prot 7 g; Carbo 38 g; Fiber 1 g;
   T Fat 9 g; 31% Calories from Fat; Chol 66 mg; Sod 212 mg.

Wenham Tea House

Double-Boiler Bread Pudding

2 slices bread, crusts removed
2 teaspoons butter, softened
1/2 cup packed brown sugar
2 eggs, beaten

2 cups milk
1/2 teaspoon vanilla extract
Salt to taste

Spread bread with butter; cut into squares. Spread brown sugar in double boiler over simmering water. Add bread pieces. Pour mixture of remaining ingredients over bread. Cook, covered, for 1 hour or until pudding tests done. Invert onto serving plate. **Yield: 4 servings.**

Nutritional information for this recipe is not available.

Tina L. Whittier

Caramel Bread Pudding

1 cup packed brown sugar
3 slices bread, cut into cubes
2 eggs, beaten

2 cups milk
1 teaspoon vanilla extract
Salt to taste

Layer brown sugar and bread cubes in buttered baking dish. Combine eggs, milk, vanilla and salt in bowl; mix well. Pour over layers. Do not stir. Set baking dish in larger pan of hot water. Bake at 350 degrees for 40 minutes. **Yield: 6 servings.**

Approx Per Serving: Cal 287; Prot 6 g; Carbo 55 g; Fiber <1 g;
  T Fat 5 g; 16% Calories from Fat; Chol 82 mg; Sod 149 mg.

Wenham Tea House

Harvest Bread Pudding

8 to 10 slices cinnamon-raisin
  bread
3 eggs, beaten
1³/₄ cups puréed pumpkin
2 cups milk

³/₄ cup sugar
¹/₂ teaspoon cinnamon
¹/₂ teaspoon pumpkin pie spice
¹/₄ teaspoon salt
¹/₂ cup raisins

Trim crusts from bread; discard. Place bread on baking sheet. Bake at 350 degrees for 5 minutes. Turn bread. Bake for 3 to 5 minutes longer or until dry. Cool to room temperature. Cut into 1-inch cubes. Mix next 7 ingredients in bowl. Stir in bread cubes. Let stand for 5 minutes. Stir in raisins. Pour into buttered 1¹/₂-quart baking dish. Bake at 350 degrees for 1 hour and 20 minutes or until knife inserted near center comes out clean. Serve warm with whipped cream. **Yield: 6 servings.**

Approx Per Serving: Cal 322; Prot 9 g; Carbo 59 g; Fiber 3 g;
  T Fat 7 g; 18% Calories from Fat; Chol 117 mg; Sod 270 mg.

Wenham Tea House

Nutmeg Sauce

2 tablespoons flour
1 cup sugar
¹/₂ teaspoon nutmeg
Salt to taste

2 cups boiling water
1 tablespoon butter
2 or 3 tablespoons rum

Mix first 4 ingredients in small saucepan. Stir in boiling water. Add butter. Cook for 5 minutes, stirring constantly. Stir in rum. **Yield: 8 servings.**

Approx Per Serving: Cal 128; Prot <1 g; Carbo 26 g; Fiber <1 g;
  T Fat 1 g; 11% Calories from Fat; Chol 4 mg; Sod 13 mg.

Wenham Tea House

Brownie Pudding

1 cup sifted flour
3/4 cup sugar
2 tablespoons baking cocoa
2 teaspoons baking powder
1/2 teaspoon salt
1/2 cup milk

2 tablespoons vegetable oil
1 teaspoon vanilla extract
3/4 cup walnuts
3/4 cup packed brown sugar
1/4 cup baking cocoa
1 3/4 cups hot water

Sift flour, sugar, 2 tablespoons baking cocoa, baking powder and salt together into bowl. Add milk, oil and vanilla; mix well. Stir in walnuts. Spoon into greased 8x8-inch baking dish. Combine brown sugar and 1/4 cup baking cocoa in bowl; mix well. Sprinkle over batter. Pour hot water over all. Bake at 350 degrees for 45 minutes. **Yield: 12 servings.**

Approx Per Serving: Cal 231; Prot 3 g; Carbo 40 g; Fiber 2 g;
    T Fat 8 g; 29% Calories from Fat; Chol 1 mg; Sod 157 mg.

Wenham Tea House

Chocolate Pudding

1 cup plus 2 tablespoons
    cornstarch
3 2/3 cups sugar
1/2 teaspoon salt
11 cups milk

1 cup black coffee
12 ounces unsweetened
    chocolate, melted
1 1/2 tablespoons vanilla extract

Combine cornstarch, sugar and salt in large double boiler. Add milk, coffee, chocolate and vanilla; mix well. Cook until thickened, stirring constantly. Simmer, covered, for 15 minutes. Serve with whipped cream. **Yield: 20 servings.**

Approx Per Serving: Cal 340; Prot 7 g; Carbo 54 g; Fiber 3 g;
    T Fat 14 g; 33% Calories from Fat; Chol 18 mg; Sod 111 mg.

Wenham Tea House

*Prevent a "skin" from forming on custards and puddings
by placing a piece of plastic wrap directly on the
surface after removing from heat.*

Cocoa Pudding

1/4 cup baking cocoa
1 cup sugar
Salt to taste

2 cups milk, scalded
1/4 cup coffee
3 tablespoons cornstarch

Combine baking cocoa, sugar and salt in double boiler. Stir in scalded milk. Mix coffee and cornstarch in bowl. Add to mixture; mix well. Cook over medium heat until thickened, stirring constantly. **Yield: 4 servings.**

Approx Per Serving: Cal 303; Prot 5 g; Carbo 63 g; Fiber 2 g;
 T Fat 5 g; 14% Calories from Fat; Chol 17 mg; Sod 54 mg.

Wenham Tea House

Date-Nut Pudding

1   8-ounce package chopped
   dates
1 teaspoon baking soda
1 cup boiling water
1 egg, beaten
1 teaspoon salt

1 cup sugar
1 tablespoon melted butter
1 cup flour
1 cup chopped pecans
1 teaspoon vanilla extract

Combine dates, baking soda and boiling water in bowl; mix well. Combine egg, salt, sugar and butter in bowl; mix well. Add flour; mix well. Add egg mixture, pecans and vanilla to date mixture; mix well. Pour into oiled and floured 8x8-inch baking dish. Bake at 350 degrees for 35 to 45 minutes or until pudding tests done. Serve warm with whipped cream or Foamy Sauce (page 153). **Yield: 12 servings.**

Approx Per Serving: Cal 236; Prot 3 g; Carbo 40 g; Fiber 2 g;
 T Fat 8 g; 30% Calories from Fat; Chol 20 mg; Sod 261 mg.

Wenham Tea House

*To reduce calories in your favorite trifle recipe, use
sliced angel food cake sprinkled with unsweetened fruit
juice instead of pound cake and sherry.*

Mock Indian Pudding

3 cups crushed cornflakes
1 egg, beaten
1 12-ounce can evaporated
    milk
1 12-ounce can water
1/3 cup molasses

1/3 cup sugar
1/2 teaspoon ginger
1/4 teaspoon cinnamon
1/4 teaspoon nutmeg
Salt to taste

Combine cornflakes, egg, milk, water, molasses, sugar, ginger, cinnamon, nutmeg and salt in bowl; mix well. Pour into greased casserole. Bake at 350 degrees for 1 hour or until knife inserted near center comes out clean. **Yield: 4 servings.**

Approx Per Serving: Cal 453; Prot 11 g; Carbo 83 g; Fiber 1 g;
    T Fat 8 g; 16% Calories from Fat; Chol 78 mg; Sod 744 mg.

Wenham Tea House

Orange-Date Pudding

12 cups milk, scalded
9 cups bread cubes
6 tablespoons butter
2 1/4 cups sugar
6 eggs
12 egg yolks
3/4 teaspoon salt
3 cups chopped dates

Grated rind and juice of 3
    oranges
Grated rind and juice of 3
    lemons
1 cup marmalade
12 egg whites
3/4 cup sugar

Combine scalded milk and bread cubes in bowl; mix well. Add butter, stirring until melted. Add 2 1/4 cups sugar, eggs, egg yolks, salt, dates, orange rind and juice and lemon rind and juice; mix well. Spoon into greased baking dish. Bake at 350 degrees for 1 1/4 hours or until set. Spread marmalade over hot pudding. Beat egg whites until soft peaks form. Add 3/4 cup sugar gradually, beating until stiff peaks form. Spread over marmalade. Bake at 400 degrees for 10 minutes longer.
Yield: 12 servings.

Approx Per Serving: Cal 819; Prot 19 g; Carbo 141 g; Fiber 5 g;
    T Fat 24 g; 25% Calories from Fat; Chol 368 mg; Sod 475 mg.

Wenham Tea House

Ozark Pudding

1 egg
3/4 cup sugar
1 tablespoon flour
1 teaspoon baking powder

1/8 teaspoon salt
1 teaspoon vanilla extract
5 small apples, peeled, chopped
1/2 cup chopped walnuts

Combine egg and sugar in mixer bowl; beat well. Mix flour, baking powder and salt together. Add to mixture; mix well. Add vanilla. Stir in apples and walnuts. Spoon into greased baking dish. Bake, covered, at 350 degrees for 35 minutes or until apples are almost tender. Remove cover. Bake until brown. Serve cold with whipped cream and additional walnuts. **Yield: 6 servings.**

Approx Per Serving: Cal 226; Prot 3 g; Carbo 40 g; Fiber 2 g;
    T Fat 7 g; 28% Calories from Fat; Chol 36 mg; Sod 112 mg.

Wenham Tea House

Rice Pudding

2 eggs, beaten
1/2 cup sugar
2 cups milk, scalded
1 teaspoon vanilla extract

1/4 teaspoon cinnamon
1 1/2 cups cooked rice
1/2 cup raisins

Combine eggs and sugar in mixer bowl; mix well. Add milk, vanilla and cinnamon; mix well. Stir in rice and raisins. Spoon into 1 1/2-quart baking dish. Bake at 350 degrees for 30 minutes. Stir well. Bake for 15 to 30 minutes longer or until knife inserted near center comes out clean. Stirring after baking for 30 minutes prevents rice and raisins from settling to bottom of pudding. **Yield: 6 servings.**

Approx Per Serving: Cal 240; Prot 6 g; Carbo 44 g; Fiber 1 g;
    T Fat 5 g; 17% Calories from Fat; Chol 82 mg; Sod 59 mg.

Wenham Tea House

*Substitute low-fat yogurt for milk and cream in
puddings and other desserts or for sour cream or
butter in uncooked frostings.*

Lemon Cream-Rice Pudding

1/2 cup uncooked rice
3 cups milk
1/2 cup sugar
Grated rind of 1 lemon
1 1/2 tablespoons lemon juice
3/4 teaspoon salt

2 tablespoons cornstarch
2 egg yolks, beaten
2 egg whites
2 teaspoons confectioners' sugar
1/4 teaspoon lemon extract

Mix rice and milk in double boiler. Cook until rice is soft, stirring occasionally. Add next 6 ingredients; mix well. Cook until thickened, stirring frequently. Pour into buttered baking dish. Cool slightly. Beat egg whites in mixer bowl until soft peaks form. Add confectioners' sugar and lemon extract alternately, beating until stiff. Spread over top of pudding. Bake at 350 degrees for 5 minutes or until meringue is brown. **Yield: 6 servings.**

Approx Per Serving: Cal 236; Prot 7 g; Carbo 39 g; Fiber <1 g;
    T Fat 6 g; 23% Calories from Fat; Chol 88 mg; Sod 338 mg.

Wenham Tea House

Butterscotch Sauce

1/2 cup packed brown sugar
1/2 cup light corn syrup
1/2 teaspoon salt

2 tablespoons butter
1 teaspoon vanilla extract

Combine brown sugar and corn syrup in saucepan. Cook over low heat for 10 minutes, stirring frequently. Add salt, butter and vanilla; mix well. **Yield: 4 servings.**

Approx Per Serving: Cal 296; Prot <1 g; Carbo 64 g; Fiber 0 g;
    T Fat 6 g; 17% Calories from Fat; Chol 16 mg; Sod 349 mg.

Wenham Tea House

Lemon Sauce

1/2 cup sugar
1 tablespoon cornstarch
1 cup boiling water
2 tablespoons butter

1 1/2 tablespoons lemon juice
Grated rind of 1 lemon
Salt to taste

Mix sugar and cornstarch in small saucepan. Stir in boiling water. Cook for 5 minutes or until thickened, stirring constantly. Stir in butter, lemon juice, lemon rind and salt. **Yield: 4 servings.**

Approx Per Serving: Cal 156; Prot <1 g; Carbo 27 g; Fiber <1 g;
    T Fat 6 g; 32% Calories from Fat; Chol 16 mg; Sod 49 mg.

Wenham Tea House

Chocolate Sauce

1½ cups sugar
1 tablespoon flour
3 tablespoons baking cocoa
1 tablespoon melted butter

¾ cup evaporated milk
1 teaspoon vanilla extract
Salt to taste

Combine sugar, flour, baking cocoa and butter with enough hot water to blend in saucepan. Simmer for 5 minutes or until thickened, stirring frequently. Add evaporated milk, vanilla and salt. Cook for several minutes longer or until of desired consistency. **Yield: 4 servings.**

Approx Per Serving: Cal 399; Prot 4 g; Carbo 83 g; Fiber 1 g;
    T Fat 7 g; 16% Calories from Fat; Chol 22 mg; Sod 77 mg.

Wenham Tea House

Foamy Sauce

3 eggs
1 cup melted butter
1½ cups sifted confectioners'
    sugar

1 tablespoon vanilla extract
3 cups whipping cream,
    whipped

Combine eggs and butter in mixer bowl; beat well. Add confectioners' sugar and vanilla; mix well. Fold in whipped cream. May serve with Date-Nut Pudding (page 149) or Chocolate Pudding (page 148). **Yield: 20 servings.**

Approx Per Serving: Cal 247; Prot 2 g; Carbo 9 g; Fiber 0 g;
    T Fat 23 g; 83% Calories from Fat; Chol 106 mg; Sod 101 mg.

Wenham Tea House

Flora Dora Sauce

2 egg yolks
½ cup sugar
2 egg whites

2 cups whipping cream,
    whipped
Sherry to taste

Combine egg yolks and sugar in mixer bowl; beat well. Beat egg whites in mixer bowl until soft peaks form. Add egg yolk mixture; beat well. Fold in whipped cream and sherry. Serve over apple crisp or puddings. **Yield: 8 servings.**

Approx Per Serving: Cal 273; Prot 3 g; Carbo 14 g; Fiber 0 g;
    T Fat 23 g; 76% Calories from Fat; Chol 135 mg; Sod 37 mg.

Wenham Tea House

Fudge Sauce

1 cup baking cocoa
3/4 cup sugar
1/2 teaspoon salt
1 tablespoon cornstarch

1/2 cup light corn syrup
1/2 cup milk
2 tablespoons butter
2 tablespoons vanilla extract

Combine baking cocoa, sugar, salt and cornstarch in double boiler; mix well. Add corn syrup and milk; mix well. Cook over hot water for 15 minutes or until thickened, stirring frequently. Stir in butter. Cool slightly. Add vanilla; mix well. May substitute 2 ounces unsweetened chocolate for baking cocoa. **Yield: 8 servings.**

Approx Per Serving: Cal 210; Prot 2 g; Carbo 41 g; Fiber 4 g;
    T Fat 9 g; 38% Calories from Fat; Chol 10 mg; Sod 176 mg.

Wenham Tea House

Cold Coffee Soufflé

1 envelope unflavored gelatin
2 cups milk
2 teaspoons instant coffee
    granules
1/3 cup sugar

3 extra large egg yolks
1/3 cup sugar
1/2 teaspoon salt
3 extra large egg whites
1/2 teaspoon vanilla extract

Soften gelatin in 1/2 cup milk in small bowl. Heat remaining 1 1/2 cups milk in double boiler. Add instant coffee, stirring until dissolved. Add gelatin mixture and 1/3 cup sugar; mix well. Cook until gelatin is dissolved, stirring frequently. Beat egg yolks in mixer bowl. Add 1/3 cup sugar and salt; beat well. Add a small amount of hot mixture to egg yolks. Stir egg yolks into hot mixture. Cook over simmering water until mixture coats a spoon, stirring frequently. Remove from heat. Cool slightly. Beat egg whites in mixer bowl until soft peaks form. Add vanilla; beat until stiff peaks form. Fold into gelatin mixture. Pour into oiled mold. Chill in refrigerator for 4 hours to overnight. The mixture will separate into 2 layers with coffee layer on bottom. Unmold onto chilled serving plate. Garnish with whipped cream and shaved semi-sweet chocolate. **Yield: 6 servings.**

Approx Per Serving: Cal 180; Prot 7 g; Carbo 26 g; Fiber <1 g;
    T Fat 6 g; 27% Calories from Fat; Chol 117 mg; Sod 242 mg.

Wenham Tea House

Cold Lemon Soufflé

1 envelope unflavored gelatin
1/2 cup cold water
3 egg yolks
1 cup sugar
1 tablespoon grated lemon rind

6 tablespoons lemon juice
3 egg whites, stiffly beaten
1 1/2 cups whipping cream,
  whipped

Soften gelatin in cold water in microwave-safe bowl. Microwave on High for several seconds or until gelatin is dissolved. Beat egg yolks and sugar in mixer bowl until light and fluffy. Add lemon rind and lemon juice; beat well. Add gelatin; beat well. Fold in egg whites and whipped cream. Spoon into parfait glasses. Chill in refrigerator for 2 hours or longer. **Yield: 6 servings.**

Approx Per Serving: Cal 381; Prot 5 g; Carbo 37 g; Fiber <1 g;
  T Fat 25 g; 57% Calories from Fat; Chol 188 mg; Sod 53 mg.

Wenham Tea House

Strawberry Mousse

3 3-ounce packages wild
   strawberry gelatin
2 1/4 cups boiling water

3 cups ice cubes
3 cups fresh strawberry halves
1 1/2 cups whipping cream

Combine gelatin and boiling water in blender container. Process at low speed for 30 seconds or until gelatin is dissolved. Add ice cubes, stirring until ice is partially melted. Reserve 18 strawberry halves. Add remaining strawberries and whipping cream to gelatin mixture. Process at high speed for 30 seconds or until well mixed. Pour into individual glasses. Chill in refrigerator for 30 minutes or until set. Garnish with reserved strawberries. **Yield: 8 servings.**

Approx Per Serving: Cal 289; Prot 4 g; Carbo 33 g; Fiber 1 g;
  T Fat 17 g; 50% Calories from Fat; Chol 61 mg; Sod 119 mg.

Wenham Tea House

*For an **Easy Coffee Mousse**, beat 1 cup whipping cream with
1 tablespoon instant coffee. Beat in 1/2 cup confectioners' sugar
and freeze in parfait glasses. Serve with crisp cookies.*

Strawberry Profiteroles

½ cup water
¼ cup butter
½ cup sifted flour
2 eggs

1 cup whipping cream
¼ cup confectioners' sugar
1 tablespoon golden rum
24 large strawberries

Bring water to a boil in saucepan. Add butter, stirring until melted. Add flour all at once, stirring until mixture forms a ball. Remove from heat. Let stand for 5 minutes. Add eggs 1 at a time, beating well after each addition. Drop dough by rounded teaspoonfuls 2 inches apart onto ungreased baking sheet to make 24 puffs. Bake at 425 degrees for 25 to 30 minutes or until puffed and golden brown. Remove to wire rack to cool completely. Beat whipping cream in bowl until soft peaks form. Add confectioners' sugar and rum gradually, beating until thick. Chill, covered, in refrigerator. Cut a slice from top of each cream puff; remove soft dough inside. Fill each with rounded teaspoonful whipped cream mixture; press a strawberry into cream. Replace tops. Chill until serving time. Place 4 puffs on each serving plate. Garnish with additional confectioners' sugar. **Yield: 6 servings.**

Approx Per Serving: Cal 320; Prot 5 g; Carbo 21 g; Fiber 3 g;
    T Fat 25 g; 69% Calories from Fat; Chol 146 mg; Sod 104 mg.

Wenham Tea House

Frozen Strawberry Squares

1 cup sifted flour
¼ cup packed brown sugar
½ cup chopped walnuts
½ cup melted butter
2 egg whites

1 cup sugar
2 cups sliced strawberries
2 tablespoons lemon juice
1 cup whipping cream, whipped

Combine flour, brown sugar, walnuts and melted butter in bowl; mix well. Spread in shallow baking pan. Bake at 350 degrees for 20 minutes, stirring several times. Sprinkle ⅔ of the baked crumbs in buttered 9x13-inch baking dish. Beat egg whites in mixer bowl until soft peaks form. Add sugar, strawberries and lemon juice alternately, beating at high speed for 10 minutes. Fold whipped cream into mixture. Spread over crumbs. Sprinkle with remaining crumbs. Freeze, covered, for 6 hours. **Yield: 15 servings.**

Approx Per Serving: Cal 246; Prot 2 g; Carbo 28 g; Fiber 1 g;
    T Fat 15 g; 52% Calories from Fat; Chol 38 mg; Sod 68 mg.

Wenham Tea House

First Church in Wenham

Cakes

Apple Cake

1/4 cup sugar
1 teaspoon cinnamon
3 cups flour
2 cups sugar
1 cup oil
1/2 cup orange juice

4 eggs
1/4 teaspoon salt
1 tablespoon baking powder
1 tablespoon vanilla extract
4 to 5 tart apples, peeled, thinly
sliced

Mix 1/4 cup sugar and cinnamon in small bowl. Combine next 8 ingredients in bowl; mix well. Layer batter, apples and cinnamon mixture 1/3 at a time in greased and floured 10-inch tube pan. Bake at 350 degrees for 1 1/2 to 2 hours or until dark brown. Cool in pan for 30 minutes. Invert onto serving plate. Serve with ice cream. **Yield: 16 servings.**

Approx Per Serving: Cal 361; Prot 4 g; Carbo 53 g; Fiber 2 g;
    T Fat 15 g; 38% Calories from Fat; Chol 53 mg; Sod 113 mg.

Irene McDougall, WVIS Member

Chocolate Fudge Cake

2 1/4 cups sifted cake flour
2 teaspoons baking soda
1/2 teaspoon salt
1/2 cup butter, softened
1 1-pound package brown
    sugar
3 eggs
3 ounces unsweetened
    chocolate, melted
1 cup sour cream

1 cup hot water
1 1/2 teaspoons vanilla extract
1 1-pound package
    confectioners' sugar, sifted
1/2 cup milk
2 teaspoons vanilla extract
4 ounces unsweetened
    chocolate
1/2 cup butter

Sift flour, baking soda and salt together. Cream 1/2 cup butter and brown sugar in mixer bowl until light and fluffy. Beat in eggs 1 at a time. Stir in melted chocolate. Beat in flour mixture and sour cream alternately. Stir in water and 1 1/2 teaspoons vanilla; batter will be thin. Pour into 2 greased and floured 9-inch cake pans. Bake at 350 degrees for 45 minutes or until layers test done. Cool in pans for 10 minutes. Remove to wire racks to cool completely. Beat confectioners' sugar, milk and 2 teaspoons vanilla in mixer bowl. Place bowl in large pan of ice water. Melt chocolate and remaining 1/2 cup butter in saucepan over low heat, stirring constantly. Stir into confectioners' sugar mixture. Beat at high speed for 2 minutes or until of spreading consistency. Frost cooled cake. **Yield: 12 servings.**

Approx Per Serving: Cal 668; Prot 6 g; Carbo 101 g; Fiber 3 g;
    T Fat 30 g; 39% Calories from Fat; Chol 105 mg; Sod 404 mg.

Wenham Tea House

Fudge Cake

1²/₃ cups flour
2 teaspoons baking soda
1 teaspoon salt
1 cup packed brown sugar
¹/₂ cup shortening
2 eggs
1 cup sour milk
2 ounces unsweetened
  chocolate

1 cup packed brown sugar
¹/₂ cup milk
1 cup sugar
2 ounces unsweetened
  chocolate
1 cup water
3 tablespoons cornstarch
¹/₂ cup butter
1 teaspoon vanilla extract

Sift flour, baking soda and salt together. Cream 1 cup brown sugar and shortening in mixer bowl until light and fluffy. Add eggs 1 at a time, beating well after each addition. Add flour mixture and sour milk alternately to creamed mixture, beating well after each addition. Combine 2 ounces chocolate, remaining 1 cup brown sugar and milk in saucepan. Cook until chocolate is melted, stirring frequently. Stir into creamed mixture. Pour into greased and floured 9x13-inch cake pan. Bake at 350 degrees for 30 minutes. Cool in pan. Combine sugar, 2 ounces chocolate, water and cornstarch in saucepan. Cook until chocolate is melted, stirring frequently. Beat in butter and vanilla. Spread over cooled cake. **Yield: 15 servings.**

Approx Per Serving: Cal 423; Prot 4 g; Carbo 64 g; Fiber 2 g;
    T Fat 19 g; 38% Calories from Fat; Chol 48 mg; Sod 340 mg.

Wenham Tea House

Chocolate-Cherry Cake

1 21-ounce can cherry pie
   filling
2 eggs, beaten
1 teaspoon almond extract
1 2-layer package chocolate
   fudge cake mix

5 tablespoons melted margarine
1 cup sugar
¹/₃ cup milk
1 cup chocolate chips

Combine pie filling, eggs and almond extract in bowl; mix well. Stir in cake mix. Pour into greased and floured 9x13-inch cake pan. Bake at 350 degrees for 35 minutes. Cool in pan. Combine margarine, sugar and milk in saucepan. Bring to a boil. Simmer for 1 minute. Stir in chocolate chips. Let stand for 5 minutes. Pour over cooled cake. **Yield: 12 servings.**

Approx Per Serving: Cal 425; Prot 4 g; Carbo 73 g; Fiber 1 g;
    T Fat 15 g; 30% Calories from Fat; Chol 36 mg; Sod 349 mg.

Alice Belknap, Chairman, Program Committee

Hershey's Syrup Cake

1 cup flour
1/2 teaspoon baking powder
1/2 teaspoon salt
1/2 cup butter, softened
1 cup sugar
4 eggs
1 teaspoon vanilla extract

1 16-ounce can Hershey's
   chocolate syrup
1/4 cup butter, softened
3 tablespoons baking cocoa
Instant coffee to taste
1/2 cup confectioners' sugar

Sift flour, baking powder and salt together. Cream 1/2 cup butter and sugar in mixer bowl until light and fluffy. Add eggs 1 at a time, beating well after each addition. Stir in vanilla. Add flour mixture and chocolate syrup alternately, beating well after each addition. Pour into greased and floured 9x13-inch cake pan. Bake at 350 degrees for 35 minutes. Combine 1/4 cup butter, cocoa, instant coffee and confectioners' sugar in bowl; beat until of spreading consistency, adding a small amount of milk if needed. Spread over cooled cake. **Yield: 15 servings.**

Approx Per Serving: Cal 271; Prot 4 g; Carbo 42 g; Fiber 1 g;
    T Fat 11 g; 36% Calories from Fat; Chol 82 mg; Sod 204 mg.
    Nutritional information does not include milk in frosting.

Wenham Tea House

Mississippi Mud Cake

1 1/2 cups flour
1/2 cup baking cocoa
1/2 cup butter, softened
2 cups sugar
4 eggs
1 cup chopped pecans
1 teaspoon vanilla extract

3 cups miniature marshmallows
1/4 cup butter
1 1-pound package
   confectioners' sugar
1/3 cup baking cocoa
1/2 cup milk
1 cup chopped pecans

Sift flour and 1/2 cup baking cocoa together. Cream 1/2 cup butter and sugar in mixer bowl until light and fluffy. Beat in eggs 1 at a time. Add flour mixture; mix well. Stir in 1 cup pecans and vanilla. Spread in buttered and floured 9x13-inch cake pan. Bake at 350 degrees for 30 minutes. Sprinkle with marshmallows. Bake for 10 minutes longer or until marshmallows melt and begin to brown. Cool in pan. Melt butter in saucepan. Beat in sifted mixture of confectioners' sugar and 1/3 cup baking cocoa alternately with milk. Stir in 1 cup pecans. Spread over cooled cake. **Yield: 15 servings.**

Approx Per Serving: Cal 550; Prot 6 g; Carbo 87 g; Fiber 3 g;
    T Fat 23 g; 36% Calories from Fat; Chol 83 mg; Sod 112 mg.

Wenham Tea House

Gingerbread

5 cups flour
2 teaspoons cinnamon
2 teaspoons cloves
4 teaspoons ginger
1 cup butter, softened

1 cup sugar
2 cups molasses
4 eggs
4 teaspoons baking soda
2 cups boiling water

Sift flour, cinnamon, cloves and ginger together. Cream butter in mixer bowl until light and fluffy. Add sugar and molasses; beat well. Add eggs 1 at a time, beating well after each addition. Stir in baking soda and boiling water. Add flour mixture; mix well. Pour into greased and floured 9x13-inch cake pan. Bake at 350 degrees for 45 minutes. **Yield: 15 servings.**

Approx Per Serving: Cal 424; Prot 6 g; Carbo 69 g; Fiber 1 g;
    T Fat 14 g; 30% Calories from Fat; Chol 90 mg; Sod 348 mg.

Wenham Tea House

Heavenly Torte

1   10-inch angel food cake
1   7-ounce jar marshmallow
    creme
1 tablespoon hot water
1¹/₂ teaspoons instant coffee
1 teaspoon vanilla extract

1 cup whipping cream, lightly
    whipped
¹/₂ ounce semisweet chocolate,
    shaved
2 tablespoons toasted slivered
    almonds

Cut cake into 3 layers. Combine marshmallow creme, water, instant coffee and vanilla in mixer bowl. Beat at low speed until well mixed; beat at high speed until fluffy. Fold in whipped cream. Spread between layers and over top of cake. Sprinkle with shaved chocolate. Top with almonds. **Yield: 12 servings.**

Approx Per Serving: Cal 260; Prot 4 g; Carbo 43 g; Fiber <1 g;
    T Fat 9 g; 29% Calories from Fat; Chol 27 mg; Sod 286 mg.

Wenham Tea House

*For an **Easy Chocolate Torte**, split 2 chocolate cake layers
and fill with mixture of 16 ounces whipped topping,
8 ounces softened cream cheese, 4 cups confectioners' sugar,
2 cups miniature chocolate chips and ¹/₂ cup nuts.*

Lemon Pound Cake

3 cups sifted flour
1/2 teaspoon baking soda
1/2 teaspoon salt
1 cup butter, softened
2 cups sugar
3 eggs
1 cup buttermilk

2 tablespoons grated lemon rind
2 tablespoons lemon juice
1   1-pound package
    confectioners' sugar
1/2 cup butter, softened
2 tablespoons grated lemon rind
1/2 cup lemon juice

Sift flour, baking soda and salt together. Cream 1 cup butter and sugar in mixer bowl until light and fluffy. Add eggs 1 at a time, beating well after each addition. Add flour mixture and buttermilk alternately to creamed mixture, ending with flour mixture and beating well after each addition. Stir in 2 tablespoons lemon rind and 2 tablespoons lemon juice. Pour into greased and floured 10-inch tube pan. Bake at 325 degrees for 1 1/4 hours or until cake tests done; do not overbake. Cool in pan for several minutes. Invert onto serving plate. Combine confectioners' sugar, 1/2 cup butter, 2 tablespoons lemon rind and 1/2 cup lemon juice in bowl; beat until of spreading consistency. Spread over top and side of cake. **Yield: 16 servings.**

Approx Per Serving: Cal 482; Prot 4 g; Carbo 77 g; Fiber 1 g;
    T Fat 19 g; 34% Calories from Fat; Chol 87 mg; Sod 268 mg.

Rosalin Wilcox, Tea House Baker

Rhubarb Upside-Down Cake

3 cups rhubarb
1 1/2 cups sifted flour
1 1/2 teaspoons baking powder
1 cup sugar
1/3 cup shortening

1/2 cup sugar
1 egg
1 teaspoon vanilla extract
1/2 cup milk

Cut rhubarb into 1/2-inch pieces. Sift flour and baking powder together. Combine 1 cup sugar and rhubarb in saucepan. Cook over medium heat for 5 to 8 minutes or until sugar is dissolved and rhubarb is tender-crisp, stirring constantly. Pour into greased 8x8-inch cake pan. Cream shortening and 1/2 cup sugar in mixer bowl until light and fluffy. Beat in egg and vanilla. Add flour mixture and milk alternately to creamed mixture, starting and ending with flour mixture and beating well after each addition. Spoon into mounds over rhubarb mixture. Bake at 350 degrees for 35 minutes. Cool. Invert onto serving plate. **Yield: 9 servings.**

Approx Per Serving: Cal 291; Prot 4 g; Carbo 51 g; Fiber 2 g;
    T Fat 9 g; 27% Calories from Fat; Chol 26 mg; Sod 71 mg.

Wenham Tea House

Jelly Roll

3/4 cup sifted cake flour
3/4 teaspoon baking powder
4 egg yolks
3/4 cup sugar, sifted
1 teaspoon vanilla extract

4 egg whites
1/4 teaspoon salt
1/4 cup confectioners' sugar
2 cups raspberry jelly
1/4 cup confectioners' sugar

Line 10x15-inch cake roll pan with buttered waxed paper. Sift flour and baking powder together. Beat egg yolks in mixer bowl. Add sugar gradually, beating constantly until mixture is creamy. Stir in vanilla. Beat in flour mixture gradually. Beat egg whites and salt in mixer bowl until stiff but not dry. Fold gently into batter. Spread in prepared pan. Bake at 375 degrees for 13 minutes or until cake tests done. Invert onto waxed paper sprinkled with 1/4 cup confectioners' sugar. Spread with jelly. Roll up from narrow end. Store, wrapped in waxed paper, until serving time. Sprinkle with remaining 1/4 cup confectioners' sugar. **Yield: 15 servings.**

Approx Per Serving: Cal 197; Prot 2 g; Carbo 45 g; Fiber <1 g;
    T Fat 2 g; 7% Calories from Fat; Chol 57 mg; Sod 76 mg.

Wenham Tea House

Pumpkin Cream Roll

3 eggs
1 cup sugar
2/3 cup pumpkin
1 teaspoon lemon juice
3/4 cup flour
1 teaspoon baking powder
2 teaspoons cinnamon
1 teaspoon ginger
1/2 teaspoon nutmeg

1/2 teaspoon salt
1/2 cup crushed walnuts
1/4 cup confectioners' sugar
16 ounces cream cheese,
    softened
3/4 cup sugar
1 egg
2 teaspoons vanilla extract
1/2 teaspoon salt

Line greased baking pan with greased waxed paper. Beat 3 eggs and 1 cup sugar in mixer bowl. Add pumpkin and lemon juice; mix well. Add flour, baking powder, cinnamon, ginger, nutmeg and 1/2 teaspoon salt; beat well. Pour onto baking pan. Sprinkle with walnuts. Bake at 375 degrees for 10 to 12 minutes or until brown. Turn onto waxed paper sprinkled with confectioners' sugar. Roll as for jelly roll. Beat cream cheese in mixer bowl until light and fluffy. Add 3/4 cup sugar, egg, vanilla and 1/2 teaspoon salt; beat until smooth. Unroll cake. Spread with cream cheese mixture; reroll. Chill until serving time. **Yield: 10 servings.**

Approx Per Serving: Cal 413; Prot 8 g; Carbo 48 g; Fiber 1 g;
    T Fat 22 g; 47% Calories from Fat; Chol 135 mg; Sod 410 mg.

Wenham Tea House

Hot Milk Sponge Cake

1½ cups cake flour
1½ teaspoons baking powder
½ teaspoon salt
¾ cup milk

2 tablespoons butter
4 eggs
1½ cups sugar
1 teaspoon vanilla extract

Sift flour, baking powder and salt together. Scald milk and butter in saucepan. Beat eggs, sugar and vanilla in mixer bowl. Add flour mixture; beat for 10 minutes. Add hot milk to batter; stir just until mixed. Pour into greased and floured 9x9-inch cake pan. Bake at 350 degrees for 45 minutes. **Yield: 12 servings.**

Approx Per Serving: Cal 199; Prot 4 g; Carbo 37 g; Fiber <1 g;
  T Fat 4 g; 20% Calories from Fat; Chol 78 mg; Sod 176 mg.

Wenham Tea House

Weary Willie Cake

1 cup flour
1 cup sugar
2 teaspoons baking powder
¼ teaspoon salt
¼ cup butter

2 ounces baking chocolate
1 egg
¾ cup milk
1 teaspoon vanilla extract
¼ cup confectioners' sugar

Sift flour, sugar, baking powder and salt together twice. Melt butter and chocolate in ovenproof dish in preheated 350-degree oven. Mix egg and milk in bowl. Add milk mixture and chocolate mixture alternately to dry ingredients, beating well after each addition. Stir in vanilla. Pour into small angel food cake pan. Bake for 35 minutes. Dust with confectioners' sugar. **Yield: 15 servings.**

Approx Per Serving: Cal 149; Prot 2 g; Carbo 23 g; Fiber 1 g;
  T Fat 6 g; 34% Calories from Fat; Chol 24 mg; Sod 116 mg.

Ruth W. Simonds, WVIS Friend

*For an easy orange frosting, use vanilla frosting
mix, substituting orange juice for water and
adding grated orange rind.*

Caramel Frosting

1¹/₃ cups packed brown sugar
¹/₄ teaspoon salt
¹/₂ cup milk
3 tablespoons butter

1 teaspoon vanilla extract
3 cups sifted confectioners' sugar

Combine brown sugar, salt and milk in saucepan. Bring to a boil. Simmer for 5 minutes or until slightly thickened. Remove from heat. Beat in butter and vanilla. Add confectioners' sugar gradually, beating until of spreading consistency. May thicken with additional confectioners' sugar or thin with additional milk if needed. **Yield: 12 servings.**

Approx Per Serving: Cal 242; Prot <1 g; Carbo 55 g; Fiber 0 g;
T Fat 3 g; 12% Calories from Fat; Chol 9 mg; Sod 87 mg.

Wenham Tea House

Creamy Chocolate Frosting

¹/₄ cup water
2 tablespoons margarine
2 ounces unsweetened
chocolate

¹/₂ teaspoon vanilla extract
2 cups sifted confectioners' sugar

Combine water and margarine in saucepan. Heat until margarine melts. Stir in chocolate and vanilla. Heat until chocolate melts. Remove from heat. Add confectioners' sugar gradually, beating until of spreading consistency. **Yield: 12 servings.**

Approx Per Serving: Cal 105; Prot 1 g; Carbo 18 g; Fiber 1 g;
T Fat 4 g; 35% Calories from Fat; Chol 0 mg; Sod 23 mg.

Wenham Tea House

Cream Cheese Frosting

6 ounces cream cheese, softened
2 tablespoons milk
1¹/₂ teaspoons vanilla extract

5 cups sifted confectioners' sugar

Combine cream cheese and milk in bowl; mix well. Stir in vanilla. Add confectioners' sugar gradually, beating until of spreading consistency. **Yield: 12 servings.**

Approx Per Serving: Cal 211; Prot 1 g; Carbo 42 g; Fiber 0 g;
T Fat 5 g; 21% Calories from Fat; Chol 16 mg; Sod 44 mg.

Wenham Tea House

Lemon-Butter Frosting

1/3 cup margarine, softened
2 cups (or more) confectioners' sugar

3 tablespoons mashed banana
1 tablespoon fresh lemon juice

Cream margarine in mixer bowl until light. Add confectioners' sugar; mix until smooth. Add banana and lemon juice; mix well. **Yield: 12 servings.**

Approx Per Serving: Cal 125; Prot <1 g; Carbo 21 g; Fiber <1 g; T Fat 5 g; 35% Calories from Fat; Chol 0 mg; Sod 59 mg.

Wenham Tea House

Creamy Frosting

1/4 cup cream cheese, softened
1 egg white, slightly beaten
1 1/2 cups confectioners' sugar

1/2 teaspoon vanilla extract
1/2 teaspoon salt

Beat cream cheese in mixer bowl. Add egg white, confectioners' sugar, vanilla and salt; beat until of spreading consistency. **Yield: 12 servings.**

Approx Per Serving: Cal 77; Prot 1 g; Carbo 15 g; Fiber 0 g; T Fat 2 g; 20% Calories from Fat; Chol 5 mg; Sod 108 mg.

Wenham Tea House

Chocolate-Butter Cream Frosting

3 tablespoons butter, softened
1 egg yolk
1 tablespoon milk
1/2 teaspoon vanilla extract

Salt to taste
1 1/4 cups sifted confectioners' sugar
1 1/2 tablespoons baking cocoa

Combine butter, egg yolk, milk, vanilla and salt in bowl; beat until smooth. Add confectioners' sugar and baking cocoa; mix well. May add a few additional drops of milk if needed for desired consistency. **Yield: 12 servings.**

Approx Per Serving: Cal 73; Prot <1 g; Carbo 11 g; Fiber <1 g; T Fat 4 g; 39% Calories from Fat; Chol 26 mg; Sod 50 mg.

Wenham Tea House

The Maples

Cookies and Pies

Butterscotch Brownies

1/2 cup melted margarine
3 cups packed dark brown sugar
4 eggs, beaten
2 cups flour
1 tablespoon baking powder

1 teaspoon salt
1 teaspoon vanilla extract
2 cups semisweet chocolate
chips

Combine margarine and brown sugar in large bowl; mix well with wooden spoon. Add eggs, flour, baking powder and salt, stirring to mix well. Stir in vanilla and chocolate chips. Pour into greased 10x15-inch baking pan. Bake at 350 degrees for 30 to 35 minutes or until edges of brownies pull away from sides of pan. May add chopped nuts. Recipe may be halved and baked in 8x8-inch baking pan. **Yield: 36 servings.**

Approx Per Serving: Cal 191; Prot 2 g; Carbo 33 g; Fiber <1 g;
    T Fat 7 g; 30% Calories from Fat; Chol 24 mg; Sod 136 mg.

Sylvia Maddix, WVIS Member

Fudge Brownies

2 ounces unsweetened
    chocolate
1/4 cup margarine
2 eggs
1 cup sugar

1/2 cup flour
1/8 teaspoon salt
1 teaspoon vanilla extract
1/2 cup chopped walnuts

Melt chocolate and margarine in saucepan, stirring constantly. Remove from heat; cool. Beat eggs in bowl. Add sugar and chocolate mixture, stirring well. Add flour, salt, vanilla and walnuts; mix well. Pour into greased 9x9-inch baking pan. Bake at 325 degrees for 35 to 40 minutes or until edges of brownies pull away from sides of pan. Do not overbake. **Yield: 16 servings.**

Approx Per Serving: Cal 141; Prot 2 g; Carbo 17 g; Fiber 1 g;
    T Fat 8 g; 47% Calories from Fat; Chol 27 mg; Sod 60 mg.

Wenham Tea House

Brownies

4 ounces unsweetened
  chocolate
3/4 cup margarine
4 eggs
2 cups sugar

1 1/2 cups flour
1 teaspoon baking powder
1 teaspoon salt
1 teaspoon vanilla extract

Melt chocolate and margarine in saucepan, stirring constantly. Remove from heat; cool. Beat eggs in bowl. Add sugar and chocolate mixture, stirring well. Add flour, baking powder, salt and vanilla; mix well. Pour into ungreased 9x13-inch baking pan. Bake at 325 degrees for 25 to 27 minutes or until edges of brownies pull away from sides of pan. May add 3/4 cup chopped nuts. **Yield: 36 servings.**

Approx Per Serving: Cal 121; Prot 2 g; Carbo 16 g; Fiber 1 g;
  T Fat 6 g; 44% Calories from Fat; Chol 24 mg; Sod 121 mg.

Wenham Tea House

Congo Bars

1 1-pound package light
  brown sugar
3/4 cup melted margarine
3 eggs
2 3/4 cups flour

1/2 teaspoon salt
2 1/2 teaspoons baking powder
1 cup semisweet chocolate chips
3/4 cup chopped pecans

Beat brown sugar and margarine in bowl. Add eggs 1 at a time, beating well after each addition. Add flour, salt and baking powder; mix well. Stir in chocolate chips and pecans. Pour into greased and floured 9x13-inch baking pan. Bake at 325 degrees for 30 minutes. **Yield: 36 servings.**

Approx Per Serving: Cal 163; Prot 2 g; Carbo 23 g; Fiber 1 g;
  T Fat 8 g; 41% Calories from Fat; Chol 18 mg; Sod 109 mg.

Wenham Tea House

Cocoa-Cheese Sandwich Cookies

2 cups flour
1/2 teaspoon salt
3/4 cup sugar
1/3 cup baking cocoa
3/4 cup butter, softened
1 egg
1 teaspoon vanilla extract

30 pecan halves
3 tablespoons butter, softened
1 tablespoon cream
3 ounces cream cheese, softened
2 cups confectioners' sugar
1/4 teaspoon salt

Beat first 7 ingredients at medium speed in mixer bowl until well mixed. Divide dough into 2 equal portions; shape into 2-inch wide rolls. Wrap in waxed paper. Chill for 2 hours or until firm. Slice dough 1/8 inch thick. Arrange on nonstick cookie sheet. Place pecan halves on half the slices. Bake at 350 degrees for 8 to 10 minutes. Cool on wire rack. Beat 3 tablespoons butter and remaining ingredients in bowl. Spread over plain cookies. Top with pecan-topped cookies. **Yield: 30 servings.**

Approx Per Serving: Cal 160; Prot 2 g; Carbo 20 g; Fiber 1 g; T Fat 9 g; 47% Calories from Fat; Chol 26 mg; Sod 113 mg.

Wenham Tea House

Abe Lincoln's Gingerbread Boys

1 cup butter, softened
1 cup sugar
1/2 cup molasses
1 teaspoon each cinnamon, nutmeg, cloves and ginger

2 eggs, well beaten
1 teaspoon vinegar
5 cups flour
1 teaspoon baking soda
Butter Frosting

Beat butter and sugar in saucepan until light and fluffy. Add molasses and spices; mix well. Bring to a boil, stirring constantly. Remove from heat; cool. Stir in eggs and vinegar. Sift flour and baking soda together. Stir into molasses mixture to form soft dough. Chill for 1 hour. Roll 1/4 inch thick on lightly floured surface. Cut with gingerbread-boy cutter. Place on greased baking sheet. Bake at 350 degrees for 8 to 10 minutes. Spread Butter Frosting over cooled cookies. Yield: 34 servings.

Butter Frosting

1/3 cup butter, softened
3 cups confectioners' sugar

1 1/2 teaspoons vanilla extract
2 tablespoons milk

Cream butter with confectioners' sugar in mixer bowl until light and fluffy. Add vanilla and milk, stirring until smooth.

Approx Per Serving: Cal 210; Prot 2 g; Carbo 33 g; Fiber <1 g; T Fat 8 g; 33% Calories from Fat; Chol 32 mg; Sod 90 mg.

Janet Tannebring, Assistant Treasurer, WVIS

Lace Cookies

1/2 cup sugar
1/2 cup flour
1/2 cup quick-cooking oats
1/2 cup melted butter
1/2 teaspoon baking powder

1 teaspoon salt
2 tablespoons cream
2 tablespoons molasses
1 teaspoon vanilla extract

Combine sugar, flour, oats and melted butter in bowl; mix well. Add baking powder, salt, cream, molasses and vanilla; mix well. Drop by teaspoonfuls 2 inches apart onto ungreased cookie sheet. Bake at 325 degrees for 10 minutes or until edges are brown. Cool on cookie sheet for several minutes; remove with spatula to wire rack to cool completely. **Yield: 32 servings.**

Approx Per Serving: Cal 56; Prot <1 g; Carbo 6 g; Fiber <1 g;
    T Fat 3 g; 53% Calories from Fat; Chol 9 mg; Sod 97 mg.

Mrs. W.L. Boyden, WVIS Member

Grasshopper Squares

1 1/2 cups sifted flour
2 cups sugar
3/4 cup plus 2 tablespoons hot
    chocolate mix
1 1/2 teaspoons salt
1 1/2 cups butter, softened
4 eggs, beaten

2 tablespoons vanilla extract
2 tablespoons light corn syrup
2 cups coarsely chopped pecans
Crème de Menthe Frosting
2 ounces unsweetened
    chocolate
2 tablespoons butter

Sift flour, sugar, hot chocolate mix and salt into bowl. Add butter, eggs, vanilla and corn syrup; mix well. Stir in pecans. Spread mixture in 9x13-inch baking pan. Bake at 350 degrees for 45 minutes; cool. Spread with Crème de Menthe Frosting. Melt chocolate and 2 tablespoons butter in saucepan, stirring constantly. Drizzle over top. Cut into squares to serve. **Yield: 36 servings.**

Crème de Menthe Frosting

2 cups sifted confectioners' sugar
1/4 cup butter, softened
2 tablespoons milk

1 teaspoon mint extract
2 ounces Crème de Menthe

Combine confectioners' sugar, 1/4 cup butter, milk, mint extract and Crème de Menthe in mixer bowl. Beat until smooth.

Approx Per Serving: Cal 246; Prot 2 g; Carbo 25 g; Fiber 1 g;
    T Fat 16 g; 56% Calories from Fat; Chol 50 mg; Sod 188 mg.

Wenham Tea House

Tropical Oatmeal Cookies

1/2 cup shortening
1/2 cup sugar
1/2 cup packed brown sugar
1 egg, beaten
1 cup crushed pineapple
1 1/2 cups oats

1 cup flour
1/2 teaspoon baking soda
1/2 teaspoon salt
1/2 teaspoon cinnamon
1/2 teaspoon nutmeg
1/2 cup chopped walnuts

Cream shortening, sugar and brown sugar in mixer bowl until light and fluffy. Beat in egg and pineapple. Add oats, flour, baking soda, salt, cinnamon, nutmeg and walnuts; mix well. Drop by teaspoonfuls onto nonstick cookie sheet. Bake at 375 degrees for 12 to 15 minutes or until golden brown. Remove to wire rack to cool. **Yield: 36 servings.**

Approx Per Serving: Cal 94; Prot 1 g; Carbo 13 g; Fiber 1 g;
T Fat 4 g; 40% Calories from Fat; Chol 6 mg; Sod 45 mg.

Jane Mallon, Wenham Exchange Office Staff

O-Henry Bars

2/3 cup butter, softened
1 cup packed light brown sugar
1/2 cup light corn syrup
1 tablespoon vanilla extract

4 cups quick-cooking oats
1 cup semisweet chocolate chips
2/3 cup peanut butter

Cream butter and brown sugar in mixer bowl until light and fluffy. Add corn syrup, vanilla and oats; mix well. Pat into ungreased 9x13-inch baking pan. Bake at 350 degrees for 15 to 18 minutes or until golden brown. Combine chocolate chips and peanut butter in top of double boiler. Cook until mixture is smooth, stirring constantly; cool slightly. Spread over prepared cookie crust. Cool completely; cut into squares. **Yield: 24 servings.**

Approx Per Serving: Cal 238; Prot 5 g; Carbo 31 g; Fiber 2 g;
T Fat 12 g; 44% Calories from Fat; Chol 14 mg; Sod 81 mg.

Anne Pearson, Gourmet Department Cook

Peanut Butter Fingers

1/2 cup margarine, softened
1/2 cup sugar
1/2 cup packed brown sugar
1 egg
1/3 cup peanut butter
1/2 teaspoon vanilla extract

1 cup flour
1 cup oats
1/2 teaspoon baking soda
1/4 teaspoon salt
1 cup chocolate chips
Peanut Butter Frosting

Cream margarine, sugar and brown sugar in bowl. Add egg, peanut butter and vanilla; mix well. Add mixture of flour, oats, baking soda and salt; mix well. Pat into 9x13-inch baking pan. Bake at 350 degrees for 20 to 25 minutes. Sprinkle with chocolate chips. Let stand for 5 minutes or until chocolate melts. Spread over baked layer. Let stand until cool. Spread Peanut Butter Frosting over chocolate layer. Let stand until frosting is firm. Cut into bars. **Yield: 36 servings.**

Peanut Butter Frosting

1/2 cup confectioners' sugar
1/4 cup peanut butter

2 to 4 tablespoons milk

Combine confectioners' sugar and peanut butter in bowl. Stir in enough milk to make of spreading consistancy.

Approx Per Serving: Cal 127; Prot 2 g; Carbo 16 g; Fiber 1 g;
    T Fat 7 g; 46% Calories from Fat; Chol 6 mg; Sod 93 mg.

Wenham Tea House

Potato Chip Cookies

1 cup butter, softened
1/2 cup sugar
1 teaspoon vanilla extract

1/2 cup crushed potato chips
1/2 cup chopped walnuts
2 cups flour

Cream butter, sugar and vanilla in mixer bowl until light and fluffy. Add potato chips, walnuts and flour; mix well. Shape mixture into 1-inch balls. Arrange on cookie sheet. Press flat with glass dipped in sugar. Bake at 350 degrees for 13 to 14 minutes or until golden brown. May substitute pecans for walnuts. **Yield: 24 servings.**

Approx Per Serving: Cal 144; Prot 2 g; Carbo 13 g; Fiber <1 g;
    T Fat 10 g; 60% Calories from Fat; Chol 21 mg; Sod 71 mg.

Lois Yeo, WVIS Member and Volunteer

Raisin Squares

3/4 cup margarine, softened
1 cup packed brown sugar
1 3/4 cups sifted flour
1/2 teaspoon salt
1/2 teaspoon baking soda
1 1/2 cups rolled oats

2 1/2 cups seedless raisins
1/2 cup sugar
2 tablespoons cornstarch
3/4 cup water
3 tablespoons lemon juice

Cream margarine and brown sugar in mixer bowl until light and fluffy. Add flour, salt, baking soda and oats; mix well. Press half the mixture into 9x13-inch baking pan. Combine raisins, sugar, cornstarch, water and lemon juice in saucepan; mix well. Cook over low heat for 5 minutes or until thickened, stirring constantly. Spoon over oat mixture. Pat remaining oat mixture over top. Bake at 400 degrees for 20 to 30 minutes. Cool in pan; cut into squares. **Yield: 36 servings.**

Approx Per Serving: Cal 143; Prot 2 g; Carbo 26 g; Fiber 1 g;
    T Fat 4 g; 25% Calories from Fat; Chol 0 mg; Sod 91 mg.

Wenham Tea House

Ranger Cookies

1 cup melted butter
1 cup sugar
1 cup packed brown sugar
2 eggs, beaten
1 teaspoon baking soda
1 teaspoon salt

1/2 teaspoon baking powder
2 cups flour
2 teaspoons vanilla extract
2 cups quick-cooking oats
2 cups crisp rice cereal

Combine butter, sugar and brown sugar in bowl; mix well. Beat in eggs, baking soda, salt and baking powder. Add flour, vanilla, oats and cereal, stirring to mix well. Drop by heaping teaspoonfuls onto cookie sheet. Bake at 350 degrees for 10 to 13 minutes or until golden brown. **Yield: 96 servings.**

Approx Per Serving: Cal 56; Prot 1 g; Carbo 9 g; Fiber <1 g;
    T Fat 2 g; 35% Calories from Fat; Chol 10 mg; Sod 59 mg.

Wenham Tea House

Mocha Shortbread for Chocolate Lovers

1 cup flour
1/3 cup sugar
2 tablespoons unsweetened
  baking cocoa

1 teaspoon instant coffee
  powder
1/2 cup butter

Combine flour, sugar, baking cocoa and coffee powder in bowl. Cut in butter until crumbly. Shape mixture into ball. Knead on lightly floured surface until dough is smooth. Pat into 8-inch circle. Prick dough deeply with fork into 16 pie-shaped wedges. Arrange on baking sheet. Bake at 325 degrees for 30 to 35 minutes or until center springs back when lightly touched. Garnish with sifted confectioners' sugar. May press dough through cookie press. **Yield: 16 servings.**

Approx Per Serving: Cal 97; Prot 1 g; Carbo 10 g; Fiber <1 g;
  T Fat 6 g; 54% Calories from Fat; Chol 16 mg; Sod 49 mg.

Dorothy Jones, Tea House Staff

Scottish Shortbread

1/4 cup butter, softened
1/2 cup sugar
1/2 cup sifted cornstarch

1/4 teaspoon salt
2 cups flour, sifted

Cream butter and sugar in mixer bowl until light and fluffy. Add cornstarch, salt and flour gradually, beating well after each addition. Divide dough into 2 equal portions. Press into two 8-inch round baking pans. Prick surface several times with fork. Bake at 350 degrees for 30 minutes or until light brown. **Yield: 12 servings.**

Approx Per Serving: Cal 160; Prot 2 g; Carbo 28 g; Fiber 1 g;
  T Fat 4 g; 23% Calories from Fat; Chol 10 mg; Sod 77 mg.

Barbara G. Clark, Exchange Book Shop Manager

To add colorful sparkle to your holiday dessert tray, roll refrigerator cookie dough into a log and mix in a combination of candied fruit and chopped almonds or walnuts. Refrigerate until firm, then slice and bake using package directions.

Spice Squares

1 cup raisins
1 cup sugar
1 cup water
1/2 cup margarine
1 teaspoon cinnamon
1/2 teaspoon cloves

1/2 teaspoon nutmeg
1/2 cup pecans
2 cups flour
3/4 teaspoon baking soda
1/8 teaspoon salt
Frosting

Combine raisins, sugar, water, margarine, cinnamon, cloves, nutmeg and pecans in saucepan; mix well. Bring to a boil. Cook for 3 minutes, stirring constantly. Remove from heat. Stir in flour, baking soda and salt. Pour into greased 9x13-inch baking pan. Bake at 350 degrees for 15 to 20 minutes. Let stand until cool. Spread Frosting over cooled layer. Cut into squares. **Yield: 24 servings.**

Frosting

1 cup confectioners' sugar
1 tablespoon milk

1/2 teaspoon vanilla extract

Beat confectioners' sugar, milk and vanilla in small bowl until smooth.

Approx Per Serving: Cal 161; Prot 2 g; Carbo 27 g; Fiber 1 g;
    T Fat 6 g; 31% Calories from Fat; Chol <1 mg; Sod 83 mg.

Wenham Tea House

Grammy's Zucchini Cookies

3/4 cup butter, softened
1 1/2 cups sugar
1 egg
1 teaspoon vanilla extract
1 1/2 cups grated zucchini
2 1/2 cups flour
2 teaspoons baking powder

1 teaspoon cinnamon
1/2 teaspoon salt
1/2 cup coarsely chopped
    almonds
1 cup chocolate chips
1 cup confectioners' sugar

Cream butter and sugar in mixer bowl until light and fluffy. Beat in egg and vanilla. Stir in zucchini. Add flour, baking powder, cinnamon and salt; mix well. Stir in almonds and chocolate chips. Drop by heaping teaspoonfuls onto greased cookie sheet. Bake at 350 degrees for 15 minutes or until light brown. Remove to wire rack to cool. Sift confectioners' sugar over tops. **Yield: 60 servings.**

Approx Per Serving: Cal 89; Prot 1 g; Carbo 13 g; Fiber <1 g;
    T Fat 4 g; 39% Calories from Fat; Chol 10 mg; Sod 50 mg.

Wenham Tea House

Sour Cream-Apple Pie

2 tablespoons flour
3/4 cup sugar
1/8 teaspoon salt
1 egg
1 cup sour cream
1 teaspoon vanilla extract
1/4 teaspoon nutmeg

2 cups chopped apples
1 unbaked 9-inch pie shell
1/3 cup sugar
1/3 cup flour
1 teaspoon cinnamon
1/4 cup butter

Sift 2 tablespoons flour, 3/4 cup sugar and salt together in large bowl. Add egg, sour cream, vanilla and nutmeg; mix well. Stir in apples. Pour into pie shell. Bake at 400 degrees for 15 minutes. Reduce oven temperature to 350 degrees. Bake for 30 minutes longer. Remove from oven. Increase oven temperature to 400 degrees. Mix remaining 1/3 cup sugar, 1/3 cup flour, cinnamon and butter in bowl. Sprinkle over pie. Bake for 10 minutes. **Yield: 6 servings.**

Approx Per Serving: Cal 510; Prot 5 g; Carbo 64 g; Fiber 2 g;
    T Fat 27 g; 47% Calories from Fat; Chol 73 mg; Sod 325 mg.

Wenham Tea House

Brownie Pie

1/2 cup chopped pecans
1 unbaked 9-inch pie shell
2 ounces unsweetened
    chocolate
1 tablespoon butter

8 ounces dark corn syrup
1/2 cup sugar
3 eggs, well beaten
1/8 teaspoon salt
1 teaspoon vanilla extract

Sprinkle pecans in pie shell. Melt chocolate and butter in saucepan. Combine corn syrup, sugar, eggs, salt and vanilla in bowl; mix well. Stir in chocolate mixture. Pour over pecans. Bake at 450 degrees for 10 minutes. Reduce oven temperature to 350 degrees. Bake for 30 minutes longer. **Yield: 6 servings.**

Approx Per Serving: Cal 494; Prot 7 g; Carbo 63 g; Fiber 3 g;
    T Fat 26 g; 46% Calories from Fat; Chol 112 mg; Sod 305 mg.

Wenham Tea House

French Silk Chocolate Pie

1/2 cup butter, softened
3/4 cup sugar
2 ounces melted unsweetened
   chocolate
1/8 teaspoon salt

1 teaspoon vanilla extract
2 eggs
1 baked 9-inch pie shell
1 cup whipping cream, whipped

Cream butter in mixer bowl, beating until light and fluffy. Add sugar gradually. Stir in chocolate, salt and vanilla. Add eggs 1 at a time, beating for 5 minutes after each addition. Pour into pie shell. Chill overnight. Top with whipped cream. Garnish with shaved bitter chocolate. Note: Be aware of possible risk of salmonella when using uncooked eggs in recipes. **Yield: 6 servings.**

Approx Per Serving: Cal 585; Prot 6 g; Carbo 41 g; Fiber 2 g;
   T Fat 47 g; 72% Calories from Fat; Chol 167 mg; Sod 395 mg.

Wenham Tea House

Coconut Custard Pie

2 eggs, beaten
2 teaspoons sugar
1/4 teaspoon grated lime rind
1 teaspoon vanilla extract

1 cup hot milk
1 1/2 cups flaked coconut
1 unbaked 9-inch pie shell

Combine eggs, sugar and lime rind in bowl; beat well. Add vanilla, milk and coconut; mix well. Pour into pie shell. Bake at 400 degrees for 25 minutes or until set. Let stand until cool. Chill until serving time. **Yield: 8 servings.**

Approx Per Serving: Cal 219; Prot 4 g; Carbo 18 g; Fiber 2 g;
   T Fat 15 g; 59% Calories from Fat; Chol 57 mg; Sod 170 mg.

Wenham Tea House

*Pies with cream or custard filling should be
cooled to room temperature and then
refrigerated to prevent spoilage.*

Grasshopper Pie

17 Hydrox cookies, crushed
1/4 cup melted butter
25 marshmallows

1/2 cup milk
3 tablespoons Crème de Menthe
1 cup whipping cream, whipped

Mix crumbs and melted butter in bowl; reserve 1/4 cup mixture. Press remaining crumb mixture in 9-inch pie plate. Combine marshmallows and milk in double boiler. Cook until marshmallows are melted. Cool slightly. Stir in Crème de Menthe. Fold in whipped cream. Spread in prepared pie plate. Sprinkle with reserved crumb mixture. Chill for 2 hours. **Yield: 6 servings.**

Approx Per Serving: Cal 480; Prot 4 g; Carbo 50 g; Fiber <1 g;
    T Fat 29 g; 55% Calories from Fat; Chol 78 mg; Sod 248 mg.

Wenham Tea House

Ice Cream Pie

2 ounces unsweetened
    chocolate
1/4 cup butter
2/3 cup sifted confectioners'
    sugar

2 tablespoons milk
1 3-ounce can coconut
1 quart peppermint ice cream,
    slightly softened

Melt chocolate and butter in double boiler over hot water. Remove from heat. Add mixture of confectioners' sugar and milk; mix well. Stir in coconut. Press in buttered pie plate. Chill until firm. Spoon ice cream into prepared pie plate. Freeze, covered with foil, until firm. Let stand for 30 minutes. **Yield: 8 servings.**

Approx Per Serving: Cal 303; Prot 4 g; Carbo 30 g; Fiber 2 g;
    T Fat 20 g; 57% Calories from Fat; Chol 46 mg; Sod 110 mg.

Wenham Tea House

*Make **Frozen Lemon Pies for-a-Crowd** with 1/2 gallon softened vanilla ice cream and 12 ounces frozen lemonade concentrate, thawed. Spoon into 3 graham cracker pie shells and freeze until firm. Garnish with whipped cream and lemon slices.*

Frozen Lemon Pie

3/4 cup vanilla wafer crumbs
3 egg yolks
1/2 cup sugar
2 tablespoons cold water
1/4 cup fresh lemon juice
Grated rind of 1 lemon

3 egg whites
1/2 cup sugar
1/2 cup whipping cream,
  whipped
1/4 cup vanilla wafer crumbs

Press 3/4 cup wafer crumbs in 9-inch pie plate. Beat egg yolks slightly in top of double boiler. Add 1/2 cup sugar, water, lemon juice and lemon rind. Cook for 5 minutes or until thickened, stirring frequently. Cool thoroughly. Beat egg whites in mixer bowl until soft peaks form. Add remaining 1/2 cup sugar gradually, beating constantly until stiff peaks form. Stir into lemon mixture. Fold in whipped cream. Spread in prepared pie plate. Sprinkle with 1/4 cup wafer crumbs. Freeze for 6 hours. Let stand for several minutes. **Yield: 6 servings.**

Approx Per Serving: Cal 307; Prot 4 g; Carbo 46 g; Fiber <1 g;
  T Fat 13 g; 36% Calories from Fat; Chol 143 mg; Sod 92 mg.

Wenham Tea House

Lemon Meringue Pie

1 1/2 cups sugar
1/2 cup cornstarch
1 1/2 cups water
3 egg yolks, slightly beaten
3 tablespoons butter
1/4 cup lemon juice

1 tablespoon grated lemon rind
1 baked 9-inch pie shell
4 egg whites
1/4 teaspoon cream of tartar
1/4 teaspoon vanilla extract
6 tablespoons sugar

Combine 1 1/2 cups sugar, cornstarch and water in saucepan. Cook over medium heat until thickened, stirring constantly. Boil for 1 minute. Stir a small amount of hot mixture into beaten egg yolks; stir egg yolks into hot mixture. Cook for 1 minute, stirring constantly. Remove from heat. Stir in butter, lemon juice and lemon rind. Pour into pie shell. Beat egg whites in mixer bowl at low speed until foamy. Add cream of tartar and vanilla. Beat at medium speed until soft peaks form. Add 6 tablespoons sugar gradually, beating constantly at high speed until stiff peaks form; do not underbeat. Spread over pie, sealing to edge. Bake at 375 degrees for 8 to 10 minutes or until meringue is golden brown. **Yield: 6 servings.**

Approx Per Serving: Cal 526; Prot 6 g; Carbo 86 g; Fiber 1 g;
  T Fat 19 g; 31% Calories from Fat; Chol 122 mg; Sod 271 mg.

Wenham Tea House

Streusel Pear Pie

1 cup sugar
2 teaspoons cinnamon
1/4 cup lemon juice
3 tablespoons quick-cooking
   tapioca
6 cups sliced peeled Bartlett
   pears

1 unbaked 9-inch pie shell
1/2 cup butter
1/2 cup packed brown sugar
1 cup flour
1/4 cup finely chopped pecans

Combine sugar, cinnamon, lemon juice, tapioca and pears in bowl. Let stand for 15 minutes. Spoon into pie shell. Cut butter into brown sugar and flour in bowl until crumbly. Pat over pear mixture. Sprinkle with pecans. Bake at 375 degrees for 50 minutes or until crust is brown. **Yield: 8 servings.**

Approx Per Serving: Cal 543; Prot 4 g; Carbo 86 g; Fiber 5 g;
   T Fat 22 g; 36% Calories from Fat; Chol 31 mg; Sod 244 mg.

Jeannie Westra, Vice President, WVIS

Deluxe Pecan Pie

3 eggs, slightly beaten
1 cup corn syrup
1 cup sugar
2 tablespoons melted butter

1 teaspoon vanilla extract
1/8 teaspoon salt
1 cup pecans
1 unbaked 9-inch pie shell

Combine eggs, corn syrup, sugar, butter, vanilla and salt in bowl; mix well. Stir in pecans. Pour into pie shell. Bake at 400 degrees for 15 minutes. Reduce oven temperature to 350 degrees. Bake for 30 to 35 minutes longer or until set. **Yield: 6 servings.**

Approx Per Serving: Cal 623; Prot 5 g; Carbo 91 g; Fiber 2 g;
   T Fat 29 g; 40% Calories from Fat; Chol 81 mg; Sod 309 mg.

Wenham Tea House

*Chill pastry for 4 to 12 hours before rolling out
to insure tender easy-to-handle pastry that
won't shrink during baking.*

Fiesta Raisin-Cranberry Pie

3 tablespoons rum
1 cup seedless raisins
2½ cups fresh cranberries
1 recipe 2-crust pie pastry

1 cup sugar
2 tablespoons cornstarch
2 teaspoons grated orange rind
¾ cup orange juice

Mix rum, raisins and cranberries in bowl. Let stand for 1 hour. Fit half the pastry into 9-inch pie plate. Spoon raisin mixture into pie plate. Combine sugar, cornstarch, orange rind and orange juice in saucepan. Cook until thickened and clear, stirring constantly. Pour over fruit. Cut remaining pastry into strips; arrange lattice-fashion on top. Bake at 425 degrees for 30 minutes. **Yield: 8 servings.**

Approx Per Serving: Cal 405; Prot 3 g; Carbo 67 g; Fiber 3 g;
    T Fat 14 g; 30% Calories from Fat; Chol 0 mg; Sod 279 mg.

Virginia Curto, WVIS Member and Volunteer

Rhubarb Pie

1 recipe 2-crust pie pastry
1¼ cups sugar
¼ cup flour
⅛ teaspoon salt

4 cups rhubarb, cut into ¼-inch
    pieces
2 tablespoons butter

Line 9-inch pie plate with half the pastry. Mix sugar, flour and salt in bowl. Add rhubarb; toss well. Place in prepared pie plate. Dot with butter. Top with remaining pastry, sealing edge and cutting vents. Bake at 425 degrees for 10 minutes. Reduce oven temperature to 350 degrees. Bake for 30 to 40 minutes or until rhubarb is tender and crust is brown. May add 1 cup crushed strawberries or pineapple to filling. **Yield: 8 servings.**

Approx Per Serving: Cal 375; Prot 3 g; Carbo 55 g; Fiber 3 g;
    T Fat 16 g; 39% Calories from Fat; Chol 8 mg; Sod 336 mg.

Wenham Tea House

*Prevent a soggy lower pie crust by brushing it
with egg white or melted butter before adding the filling.*

Strawberry Cream Pie

1 5-ounce can evaporated milk
1 3-ounce package strawberry
   gelatin
1/2 cup boiling water
3/4 cup sugar
1 tablespoon lemon juice
1/2 cup crushed strawberries
1/8 teaspoon salt
1 baked 9-inch pie shell
1 cup whipping cream, whipped

Chill evaporated milk for 24 hours. Dissolve gelatin in boiling water in bowl. Add sugar, lemon juice and strawberries. Chill until partially set. Whip evaporated milk in mixer bowl until stiff. Whip into gelatin mixture. Stir in salt. Spoon into pie shell. Top with whipped cream. Garnish with whole strawberries. **Yield: 8 servings.**

Approx Per Serving: Cal 357; Prot 4 g; Carbo 42 g; Fiber 1 g;
    T Fat 20 g; 49% Calories from Fat; Chol 46 mg; Sod 235 mg.

Wenham Tea House

Glazed Berry Pie

1 cup sugar
2 tablespoons cornstarch
1/8 teaspoon salt
13/4 cups cold water
1 3-ounce package strawberry
   gelatin
3 pints fresh strawberries
1 baked 9-inch pie shell
1 cup whipping cream, whipped

Combine sugar, cornstarch and salt in saucepan. Stir in cold water. Cook until clear, stirring constantly. Remove from heat. Stir in gelatin until dissolved. Chill until partially set. Place strawberries in pie shell. Spoon gelatin mixture over strawberries. Chill until serving time. Top with whipped cream. **Yield: 8 servings.**

Approx Per Serving: Cal 392; Prot 4 g; Carbo 55 g; Fiber 3 g;
    T Fat 19 g; 42% Calories from Fat; Chol 41 mg; Sod 218 mg.

Jeanne A. Niederer, Wenham Exchange

*Patch tears in pastry with a bit of pastry and a touch
of ice water rather than by rerolling it.*

Nana Johnson's Squash Pie

1 recipe 1-crust pie pastry
2/3 cup sugar
2 teaspoons flour
1/2 teaspoon salt
1/2 teaspoon cinnamon
1/2 teaspoon nutmeg

1/2 teaspoon ginger
2 eggs, slightly beaten
1 1/4 cups strained cooked
   butternut squash
1 cup warm milk

Line pie plate with pastry. Bake at 400 degrees until brown. Combine sugar, flour, salt, cinnamon, nutmeg and ginger in bowl; mix well. Beat in eggs. Add squash; mix well. Stir in milk. Strain into prepared pie plate. Bake at 375 degrees for 50 to 60 minutes or until wooden pick inserted in center comes out clean. **Yield: 8 servings.**

Approx Per Serving: Cal 232; Prot 4 g; Carbo 32 g; Fiber 2 g;
   T Fat 10 g; 38% Calories from Fat; Chol 57 mg; Sod 302 mg.

Martha Wildes Carr, WVIS Member

Walnut Crumb Crust

1/2 package pie crust mix
1/4 cup packed light brown
   sugar
3/4 cup finely chopped walnuts

1 ounce unsweetened
   chocolate, grated
1 teaspoon vanilla extract
1 tablespoon (or more) water

Combine pie crust mix, brown sugar, walnuts and chocolate in bowl; mix well. Stir in vanilla and water. Press into well greased 8-inch pie plate. Bake at 375 degrees for 15 minutes. **Yield: 6 servings.**

Approx Per Serving: Cal 295; Prot 5 g; Carbo 29 g; Fiber 2 g;
   T Fat 20 g; 57% Calories from Fat; Chol 0 mg; Sod 177 mg.

Wenham Tea House

*Make **Basic Pastry** in the food processor. Process 2 cups flour, 1/2 teaspoon salt and 2/3 cup cold margarine until of fine-crumb consistency. Drizzle in 5 1/2 tablespoons water and process until mixture forms ball. Chill for 15 minutes. May store in refrigerator for up to 8 days.*

NUTRITIONAL GUIDELINES

The editors have attempted to present these family recipes in a form that allows approximate nutritional values to be computed. Persons with dietary or health problems or whose diets require close monitoring should not rely solely on the nutritional information provided. They should consult their physicians or a registered dietitian for specific information.

Abbreviations for Nutritional Analysis

Cal — Calories	Dietary Fiber — Fiber	Sod — Sodium
Prot — Protein	T Fat — Total Fat	gr — gram
Carbo — Carbohydrates	Chol — Cholesterol	mg — milligrams

Nutritional information for these recipes is computed from information derived from many sources, including materials supplied by the United States Department of Agriculture, computer databanks and journals in which the information is assumed to be in the public domain. However, many specialty items, new products and processed foods may not be available from these sources or may vary from the average values used in these analyses. More information on new and/or specific products may be obtained by reading the nutrient labels. Unless otherwise specified, the nutritional analysis of these recipes is based on all measurements being level.

* **Artificial sweeteners** vary in use and strength so should be used "to taste," using the recipe ingredients as a guideline. Sweeteners using aspartame (NutraSweet and Equal) should not be used as a sweetener in recipes involving prolonged heating which reduces the sweet taste. For further information, refer to package information.
* **Alcoholic ingredients** have been analyzed for the basic ingredients, although cooking evaporates the alcohol thus decreasing caloric content.
* **Buttermilk, sour cream** and **yogurt** are the types available commercially.
* **Cake mixes** which are prepared using package directions include 3 eggs and 1/2 cup oil.
* **Chicken**, cooked for boning and chopping, has been roasted; this method yields the lowest caloric values.
* **Cottage cheese** is cream-style with 4.2% creaming mixture. Dry-curd cottage cheese has no creaming mixture.
* **Eggs** are all large. (To avoid raw eggs that may carry salmonella as in eggnog or 6-week muffin batter, use an equivalent amount of commercial egg substitute.)
* **Flour** is unsifted all-purpose flour.
* **Garnishes**, serving suggestions and other optional additions and variations are not included in the analysis.
* **Margarine** and **butter** are regular, not whipped or presoftened.
* **Milk** is whole milk, 3.5% butterfat. Lowfat milk is 1% butterfat. Evaporated milk is whole milk with 60% of the water removed.
* **Oil** is any type of vegetable cooking oil. Shortening is hydrogenated vegetable shortening.
* **Salt** and other ingredients to taste as noted in the ingredients have not been included in the nutritional analysis.
* If a choice of ingredients has been given, the nutritional analysis reflects the first option. If a choice of amounts has been given, the nutritional analysis reflects the greater amount.

INDEX

SOUPS, COLD
Blueberry Soup, 54
Chilled Raspberry-Lime Rickey
Soup, 55
Cold Spinach Soup, 57
Cold Strawberry Soup, 55
Cold Vegetable Soup, 56
Cucumber Soup, 54
Gazpacho Soup, 54
Tomato Mist, 55

SOUPS, HOT
Carrot Soup, 57
Christmas Soup, 56
Cream of Mushroom Soup, 57
French Onion Soup, 58
Mock Turtle Soup, 56
Seafood Chowder, 58
Spinach Soup, 59
Squash Soup, 59
Summer Harvest Soup, 60
Tomato Toddy, 60
Tomato-Zucchini Soup, 60

STRAWBERRY
Frozen Strawberry Squares, 156
Glazed Berry Pie, 183
Strawberry Cream Pie, 183
Strawberry Mousse, 155
Strawberry Profiteroles, 156

TEA
Brew a Perfect Cup of Tea, 23
Kinds of Tea, 23
Tea Packs a Punch, 25

TEA ROOM SANDWICHES
Almond-Chicken Filling, 28
Bon Chees, 26
Breadless Roll, 29
Cheese Sandwich, 26
Chutney Cream Cheese, 30
Cinnamon Toast, 26
Cooked Shrimp Filling, 28
Cream Cheese and Olive, 28
Crushed Pineapple and Chopped
Pecan Filling, 28
Cucumber Sandwiches, 29
Curried Chicken with Walnut
Topping, 28
Dilled Salmon Cream Cheese
Spread, 30
Egg and Watercress Sandwiches, 30
Filled Cream Puffs, 30
Honey and Orange Rind Filling, 28
Mushroom Rolls, 29
Rolled Asparagus, 29
Shrimp with Celery Topping, 28
Smoked Salmon Pinwheel
Sandwich, 29
Toasted Lobster Sandwich, 26
Toasted Salmon Sandwiches, 26
Tomato and Basil Topping, 28
Tuna Capers Sandwiches, 30

TURKEY
Baked Turkey Croquettes, 95
Swiss Turkey-Ham Bake, 78
Topnotch Turkey Loaf, 95

VEGETABLES
Baked Mushrooms, 113
Broccoli with Sour Cream Sauce, 110
Cauliflower and Mushroom
Casserole, 111
Corn Casserole, 112
Country Potato Casserole, 113
Creamy Potato Puff, 114
Do-Ahead Mashed Potatoes, 114
Eggplant and Mushroom
Casserole, 112
French Onion Casserole, 113
Green Beans Oriental, 110
Party Potatoes, 114
Refrigerator Mashed Potatoes, 115
Rolled Asparagus, 29
Sprouts Emerald Isle, 111
Tomato Pie, 115
Tomato-Zucchini Scallop, 116
Turnip Casserole from Finland, 116

Wenham Tea House Cookbook

Please send me _____ copies of the *Wenham Tea House Cookbook*

Wenham Tea House Cookbook	@ $15.95 each	_____
Shipping and Handling	@ $ 3.50 each	$_____
Massachusetts residents add 5% sales tax		$_____
	Total	$_____

Name _____

Address _____

City/State/Zip _____

Make checks payable to:

Wenham Village Improvement Society
4 Monument Street
Wenham, MA 01984
(508) 468-1235